NOT-FOR-PARENTS

# EUROPE

# Everything you ever wanted to know

Clive Gifford

# CONTENTS

THIS BOOK'S BETTER THAN THE WEB!

WHOOPS, WATCH OUT BELOW!

WHO'S YOUR FAVOURITE EUROPEAN LEADER?

NAPOLEON BONE-APART, OF COURSE!

TURN THE PAGE... THAT'S AN ORDER!

# NOT-FOR-PARENTS

**THIS IS NOT A GUIDEBOOK.** And it is definitely Not-for-parents.

**IT IS THE REAL, INSIDE STORY** about one of the world's most colourful continents – Europe. In this book you'll read about **bizarre** pastimes from **wok racing** and mobile phone hurling to grown-up food fights and **rotten shark chomping**.

You'll learn the gruesome facts about some of history's most **bloodthirsty** rulers and can check out sculptures made of **human bones**, the world's **biggest pizza**, **ultra-cool ice hotels**, and a metal-munching Frenchman.

This book shows you a **EUROPE** your parents probably don't even know about.

# NATIONS OF EUROPE

Every nation in Europe has its own culture, traditions and laws. And some are downright odd. It's illegal, for example, to feed pigeons in Venice, Italy, flush toilets after 10pm in Swiss apartments or tune pianos at midnight in Germany. Neither can you name a pig Napoleon in France or build sandcastles on the beach at Eraclea in Italy.

**Short and Swede**
Whilst there is a place in northern France called Y, Norway and Sweden take the prize for having the shortest placenames. There are three different villages all called Å in the county of Troms in northern Norway, which must get confusing. Sweden has an Å of its own – and another village called Ö.

The place with the longest name in Europe is in Wales, UK… [deep breath]…

Llanfairpwllgwyngyllgogerychwyrndrobwllllantysiliogogogoch

It means… [another deep breath]… 'Saint Mary's Church in the hollow of the white hazel near a rapid whirlpool and the Church of St Tysilio of the red cave.'

**Banding together**
A whole bunch of European countries have grouped together to form the European Union. They share a number of laws and 17 of these countries all use the same money, the Euro. There were around 15.7 billion Euro banknotes in use at the start of 2013. That's a lot of lolly.

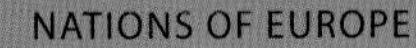

**Name change**
Istanbul was once called Constantinople and before that Byzantium. It's the capital city of Turkey and the only capital city that spans two continents. Its western side is in Europe but if you take a short ferry ride or cross a bridge over the Bosphorus, you'll find yourself in Asia.

Finland
Sweden
Norway
Estonia
Latvia
Russia
Denmark
Lithuania
Belarus
Poland
Netherlands
Ukraine
Belgium
Germany
Czech Republic
Luxembourg
Slovakia
Moldova
Liechtenstein
Austria
France
Hungary
Switzerland
Romania
Slovenia
Croatia
Bosnia and Herzegovinia
Italy
Serbia
Monaco
San Marino
Bulgaria
Andorra
Montenegro
Kosovo
Albania
Vatican City
Turkey
Greece
Cyprus

WANT MORE?

Check out the flags of Europe ✯ www.nationsonline.org/oneworld/flags_of_europe.htm

# FOOD FIGHTS

Every kid loves a good food fight and it turns out quite a few adults in Europe do, too. Here are three messy festivals that prove the point.

COME ON, YOU'RE BEHIND. TRY TO KETCHUP!

### Paint the town red

The sleepy town of Buñol near Valencia, in Spain, has a population of 9000. But on the last Wednesday in August, numbers swell to five or six times that. All the visitors come for La Tomatina – the mother of all food fights.

A tomato thrower makes a splash in a slushy street.

Tomatoes are slightly acidic, which means they help to remove dirt. So once the streets are hosed down they are left sparkling clean.

### Take that splat!

An hour before midday, giant trucks trundle into town and dump around 150,000 old tomatoes. Everyone grabs what they can and throws tomatoes into the crowd. That's 40 tonnes (44 tons) of tomatoes squished and squashed in just 60 minutes of mayhem. It's Tomatageddon!

### Hip, hip, purée

An hour later a rocket fires to tell everyone the fun is over. The streets are left swimming in tomato slush, and friendly locals, along with the fire service, hose down the juicy revellers.

## A JUICY BATTLE

The Battle of the Oranges in the Italian town of Ivrea started centuries ago and is said to commemorate the victory of villagers over an evil landowner. Today, around 3000 people from the town do battle on foot or in horse-drawn carts. Many wear medieval clothing.

OF ALL THE WAYS TO GET MY DAILY DOSE OF VITAMIN C.

**Messy meringue wars!**
The Spanish town of Vilanova i La Geltrú is famous for *xató* – a salad of fish and vegetables. However, in February of each year, the diet isn't so healthy. As part of a festival, the townsfolk hurl masses of meringues at each other. Other sweets are also thrown out into the crowds, which are packed with sweet-toothed kids.

**Fruitful fight**
Around 57,000 crates of oranges are shipped in for the Ivrea battle. These food fighters are serious! The end result is juice-soaked crowds and streets covered in pulp and peel.

WANT MORE?

Meringue Wars ✯ www.catalunyaonline.cat/carnavalvilanova/idioma_en.html

# VLAD THE BAD

During the Middle Ages, there were many bad-boy rulers of kingdoms who thought nothing of slicing up rivals or plundering foreign villages and towns. But few were as brutal as Vlad III Dracul, also known as Vlad Tepes. Vlad was born into a powerful family. His father, Vlad II Dracul, ruled the kingdom of Wallachia (now in Romania) and was often at war with the mighty Ottoman Empire.

Vlad III Dracul

It's believed Vlad III had 20,000 to 100,000 people impaled on spikes!

In 1442, when Vlad was 11, his Dad sent him to the court of the Ottoman ruler, Murad II, as a hostage!

**It's a stick up!**
Vlad III didn't like giving the enemy an honourable burial. Instead, he preferred to stick their dead heads on posts as a warning. Some victims were executed by being dropped onto sharpened stakes. This is how he got his nickname, Vlad the Impaler. During his reign, fields became full of impaled victims. Vlad even ate his dinner outside amid the grisly scenes.

## WARRING WALLACHIA

Vlad III came to power in 1448 after his father was killed and rebels had blinded (with a red-hot poker) then buried alive his half-brother, Mircea. Vlad's first spell in charge didn't last long but he returned in 1456 and ruled with an iron fist from his capital at Târgovişte.

### Reign of terror

One legend tells that Vlad left a solid gold chalice or cup in the centre of a public square for years. Anyone could have picked it up and stolen it – but no one dared to as the punishment for theft was, of course, death.

Vlad's head carved in stone

### Hats off to Vlad

Many stories are told of Vlad III's cruelty. Once, foreign messengers visited his court in Târgovişte but refused to remove their hats. Angry Vlad had his guards nail their hats onto their heads.

**Double ouch!**

### Watch your back

When he wasn't warring with the Ottomans, Vlad was wiping out rebellions and threats to his own power. He was imprisoned several times, and died in battle at the age of 45. The Ottomans carried Vlad's head back to Istanbul to reassure everyone that their arch enemy's deadly days were over.

### Stoking the imagination

Bad Vlad's bloodthirsty ways, his birthplace of Transylvania and his name Dracul may have been the inspiration behind Bram Stoker's famous 1897 vampire tale, *Dracula*.

How were Vlad and Dracula different? ✯ www.vladtheimpaler.com

# WHAT AN ICE PLACE TO VISIT

Deep inside the Arctic circle, 20km (12mi) from Sweden's most northern city, Kiruna, lies the village of Jukkasjärvi. In 1990, a French artist, Jannot Derid, held an exhibition of art in a large igloo. One night, visitors couldn't find anywhere to stay. So they kipped inside the icy igloo in sleeping bags laid on top of reindeer skins. A local businessman, Yngve Bergqvist, had a brainwave… what if we built a hotel out of ice?

The hotel bar is made from 40-50 tonnes (44-55 tons) of clear ice kept at -5°C (23°F). Even the glasses and bowls are made from ice.

**Hit hotel**
As crazy as it sounds, the ice hotel was a huge hit and has been open for business ever since. Actually, a different hotel opens every summer because each one melts back into the nearby River Torne and has to be rebuilt.

Colourful drinks are served in glasses carved out of ice.

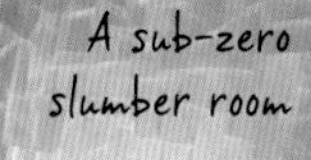

A sub-zero slumber room

**Ice accommodation**
Every year as winter comes, a large team of builders begin work. Blocks of ice from the River Torne are moved into place. Machines pump and spray snow onto frames to form rooms for over 100 guests. The completed hotel features a large hall and reception area, a bar and even a church.

## ARCTIC ART

Around 50 ice artists from all over the world descend on Jukkasjärvi. They begin work on the interior which includes ice chairs and tables, beds and ornate walls. Ice is sawn, chiselled and heated to form astonishing sculptures.

**Snow sights**
You'll need a snowmobile, motorsled or a sled pulled by husky dogs to take in the sights. The area is one of the best in Europe for viewing the astonishing northern lights, or aurora borealis, which appear in the night sky.

Aurora borealis

WANT MORE?

See and read more ✯ www.icehotel.com

# A MEAL FIT FOR A QUEEN

It's June 1889 and Italian cook Raffaele Esposito has a king-sized problem. King Umberto I and his wife, Queen Margherita di Savoia, are visiting Naples. Esposito has been invited to serve them dinner. Pizzas had only recently become popular, and it was said that the Queen had never tasted this simple dish before. Esposito was desperate to make her a special one.

King Umberto I

**Margherita's a winner**
According to legend, Esposito made three different pizzas. The one the Queen liked the most was topped with tomato slices, mozzarella cheese and basil leaves to represent the red, white and green of the Italian flag. The pizza, named in the Queen's honour, caught on in Naples and spread throughout Italy.

By Italian law, a real Margherita pizza must have thinly sliced San Marzano tomato, dough rested for six hours and be cooked in a wood-fired oven.

## PIZZA THE ACTION

The delights of Margherita pizzas spread to the United States via Italian immigrants and US soldiers returning home after World War II. Today, Americans eat more pizza than any other nation – three billion per year!

Queen Margherita

South Africa held the world record for the largest pizza until 2012, when five Italian chefs brought the record home with a 40m-wide whopper (130ft)!

GIANT PIZZA INGREDIENTS

4 tonnes (4.4 tons) tomato sauce
4 tonnes (4.4 tons) mozzarella cheese
190kg (419lb) vegetable oil
675kg (1488lb) margarine
250kg (550lb) sea salt
125kg (275lb) Parmesan cheese

I KNOW I ORDERED THE EXTRA-LARGE BUT THIS IS RIDICULOUS!

Germans top the Euro pizza-eating league, gobbling 250,000 tonnes (275,000 tons) of frozen pizza every year.

Spain
76,000 tonnes
(83,700 tons)

France
83,000 tonnes
(91,500 tons)

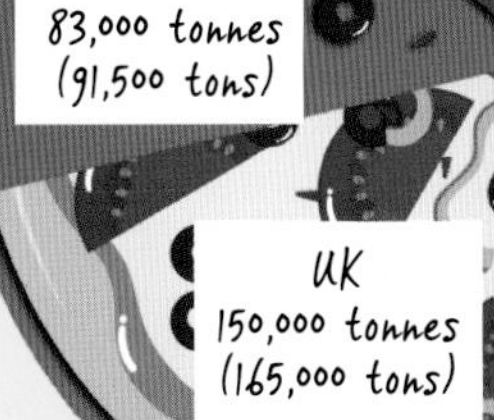

Germany
250,000 tonnes
(275,000 tons)

UK
150,000 tonnes
(165,000 tons)

**Speedy pizza**

This clever pizza vending machine makes a fresh pizza base from scratch, covers it in tomato sauce and a choice of toppings, before baking it in less than two minutes!

WANT MORE?

**The 40-m pizza (130ft) weighed over 20 tonnes (22 tons) and took two days to bake!**

# CONFESS OR DIE!

In many parts of medieval Europe, if you weren't a 100% faithful follower of the Catholic Church, you'd better watch out. The Church was boss and anyone who opposed or practised other faiths was a heretic. Inquisitions (organised church courts) questioned anyone suspected of heresy and punished those found guilty. These trials happened throughout medieval Europe and the most infamous was the Spanish Inquisition.

*Trial for heresy during the Spanish Inquisition*

**Isabella and Ferdinand**

### Worship warning

Set up in 1478 by King Ferdinand and Queen Isabella, the Spanish Inquisition was out to get you, especially if you were a Jew. Thousands of Jews were either punished or forced out of Spanish territory. Even good Catholics fell foul of the Inquisition.

IS IT JUST ME OR IS IT HOT IN HERE?

### RELAX!

Sentences varied from hefty fines or being whipped to life imprisonment or 'relaxation'. Although the last sentence was anything but relaxing – it meant you were burned at the stake. More than 2000 people died this way in Spain.

Once you were 12, if a girl, or 14, if a boy, you could be interrogated by the Spanish Inquisition.

## Torturous ways

Some who denied doing anything wrong faced horrific torture. The Inquisition had a terrifying range of methods to make them confess. Each was more horrible than the last.

*The water cure was pouring up to 8 litres (14 pints) of water through a cloth into someone's mouth to give the sensation of drowning.*

ARE YOU PULLING MY LEG?

*Bodies were stretched on the rack until bones snapped and joints dislocated.*

*An iron chain was tightened across the chest to cut into flesh. Thumbscrews (left) were tightened until thumb bones cracked.*

*A victim was lashed to a wheel which was then turned over a burning fire pit. They were slowly roasted to within an inch of their life.*

**Far from innocent**

The first church leader to allow torture (in 1252) was named Innocent – Pope Innocent IV to be precise. Many torture victims confessed to things they hadn't done or died during torture.

WANT MORE?

Read more ✯ http://encyclopedia.kids.net.au/page/sp/Spanish_Inquisition

# PET RESCUE

For over 900 years, travellers through the treacherous Great St Bernard Pass in Switzerland could find refuge in a small travellers' retreat. It was run by monks and called St Bernard's Hospice. Dogs bred and kept by the monks became well known for their mountain rescues. This turned them into one of the most recognisable breeds of big pooches – the St Bernard.

**High-altitude route**
The Great St Bernard Pass allowed travel from Italy to France. Ancient Roman armies used it to invade Gaul (France) almost 2000 years ago. In winter, the 80km-long pass (49mi) could be deadly. It had no trees for firewood or shelter and 10m-deep snow (33ft) in places.

Statue of St Bernard

## EMPTY KEG

St Bernard dogs are often pictured with a barrel of brandy around their necks. But it's a myth that they were ever worn. An 1820 painting by Edwin Landseer featured them and the idea caught on.

## BIG BEASTS

St Bernard dogs stand up to 90cm (35in) tall at their shoulders. They have giant heads with powerful jaws. When they shake their heads, their great jowls can cover you in slobber... URGH!

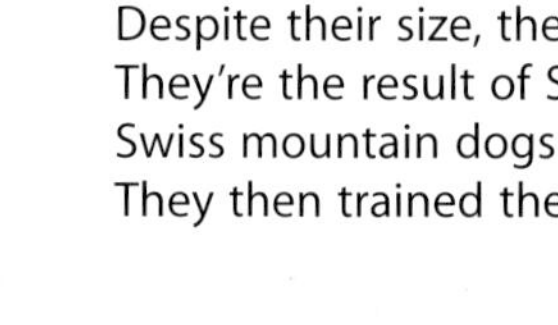

## THESE DOGS ARE PUSSYCATS!

Despite their size, these dogs are very friendly and gentle. They're the result of St Bernard's Hospice monks breeding Swiss mountain dogs with other species of king-sized canines. They then trained the dogs to rescue lost or injured travellers.

The hospice was founded by Bernard of Menthon in around 1050. He was made a saint in 1681.

HOPE THEY'VE BROUGHT ME A TASTY BONE.

**Saved by slobber**

The rescue dogs could sniff out a person trapped under many metres of snow. Whenever they found a victim, one would head back to alert humans. Meanwhile, one or more St Bernards lay beside the casualty, keeping them warm and offering a friendly lick.

**Well-kept pets**

St Bernard dogs last made a lifesaving rescue in the Alps in 1897. But dogs were bred and kept as pets at the hospice until 2004. Today, some of the dogs return to stay with the monks at the hospice during the summer.

WANT MORE?

**Canine hero Barry (1800–14) rescued more than 40 people on the pass.**

## LI'L LIECHTENSTEIN

Liechtenstein is bordered by Switzerland and Austria, and hasn't had an army or navy since 1868. Any serious criminal is imprisoned in Austria. There's no airport but it does have a postage stamp museum in a single room in the capital, Vaduz.

Independent: 1806
Area: 160sq km (62sq mi)
Population: 36,000

**Country for rent**
Since 2011, you can actually hire the entire country of Liechtenstein for US$70,000 per night. For that you get your own personalised currency and street sign as well!

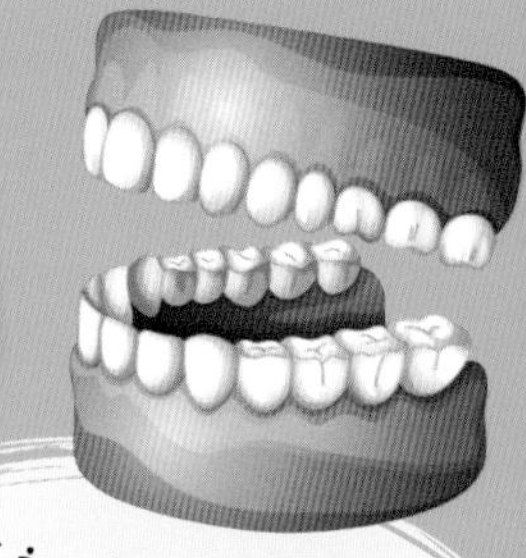

Liechtenstein is the world's leading producer of false teeth!

# BLINK AND YOU'LL MISS 'EM

In Europe's long, long history, mighty empires have risen, fallen and disappeared from maps. Yet some small territories have survived. So, get out your atlas and magnifying glass to view the four tiniest nations of Europe. Known as micro-states, they are so small you could walk across two of them in less than half an hour and cycle across the others in 60 minutes max!

## VERY, VERY SMALL VATICAN CITY

Vatican City is entirely surrounded by the Italian capital city, Rome. It is home of the Pope, who is head of the worldwide Catholic Church. Vatican City houses hundreds of amazing works of art. It's smaller than New York's Central Park, but has its own helipad and train station.

Independent: 1929
Area: 0.4sq km (0.2sq
Population: 840

A Swiss Guard, protector of the Pope and his residence.

St Peter's Basilica

## MINUSCULE MONACO

Monaco is named after the monk's clothing Francesco Grimaldi wore the night he seized its fortress in 1297. Members of the Grimaldi family have ruled it ever since. Monaco's now home to many rich businesspeople and racing drivers, partly because they don't have to pay income taxes.

The Grotte de l'Observatoire in Monaco is the only cave in Europe where the temperature rises as you go deeper inside it.

Independent: 1297
Area: 2sq km (0.8sq mi)
Population: 36,400

Independent: 301 AD
Area: 61sq km (24sq mi)
Population: 32,400

## SERIOUSLY SMALL SAN MARINO

San Marino is one of the oldest countries in the world. Surrounded by Italy, you can see the entire country from the top of its one peak, Mount Titano. Its Curiosity Museum includes a petrol-powered hairdryer, a watch to wear on your nose and the world's biggest crab.

If that's not to your taste, how about San Marino's Museum of Torture with more than 100 medieval terror and torture devices?

WANT MORE?

**Vatican City's cash machine instructions are in Latin.**

# BIG BANG

Alfred Nobel

On 13 April 1888, Swedish explosives maker Alfred Nobel (1833–96) woke up, picked up a French newspaper and read that he had died. It was quite a shock. He felt perfectly fine. The newspaper had published Alfred's life story. It called him 'a merchant of death' for inventing the powerful explosive, dynamite. Alfred vowed to do something to make people remember him more fondly.

**Explosive ending**

A chemist and engineer, Nobel was fascinated by explosives. He was particularly interested in nitroglycerine which was very unstable and could explode without warning. One such explosion killed Alfred's brother, Emil, in 1864. It left him determined to find ways to make nitroglycerine safer.

Nitroglycerine molecule

**A dynamite idea**

Nobel experimented with nitroglycerine on a barge in the middle of Lake Mälaren, Sweden. In 1866, he created a mixture of the explosive and a fine crumbly rock called *kieselgur*. It made a paste that could be shaped into rods which he called dynamite.

**Where there's a will**
Nobel died in 1896. In his will he left most of his fortune to give as prizes to people who made major advances in physics, chemistry, literature, peace and medicine. A sixth prize in economics was added in 1969.

**Prize money**
The first Nobel Prizes were awarded in 1901. Wilhelm Röntgen of Germany won the first Nobel Prize for Physics for his discovery of X-rays. Today's winners receive a cool £784,100 (US$1.2 million).

In 1970, dynamite was used to blow up a dead sperm whale. Too much was used, resulting in chunks of whale flying 240m (787ft) and crushing parked cars!

WANT MORE?

More Nobel Prize facts ✯ www.nobelprize.org/nobel_prizes/nobelprize_facts.html

In 2002, six Moroccan border guards kitted out with tents, a radio and two flags 'captured' Isla del Perejil from Spain. They renamed it Leila, but didn't stay for too long. A week later, Spanish forces recaptured the island without a struggle. It's not the only strange dispute over territory to occur in modern Europe.

**Herb island**

Isla del Perejil means Parsley Island in Spanish because that's what mainly grows on it. The island's only creatures are lizards, insects and the occasional goat shipped over from Morocco to nibble on its plants and herbs.

# STRANGE INVASIONS

**Meet the royals**

Here's Prince Roy and Princess Joan in 1966. Bow down to the mighty rulers of Sealand.

## SEALAND

Britain built concrete sea forts to protect its coasts during World War II. All were torn down after the war except Fort Roughs Tower, in the North Sea. It lies about 11.5km (7mi) off the coast of England. In 1966, Roy Bates bought the sea fort, claiming it as a new nation called Sealand.

## FEELING PEAKY

In 1861, Italy formed from a number of smaller states. At the time France and Italy agreed to share ownership of the highest mountain peak in the Alps – Mont Blanc. Sounds fine, except that some French maps have since been sneakily redrawn to show the peak inside France.

## ROCKALL

This brilliantly named outcrop rises around 20m (66ft) above the North Atlantic Ocean. Rockall's ownership is challenged by four European powers: Iceland, Ireland, Denmark and Britain. It's now up to the United Nations to settle the argument.

**Lost In Liechtenstein**

In 2007, 170 Swiss soldiers got lost during training and found themselves 1.5km (0.9mi) inside Liechtenstein. The Swiss quickly apologised for the accidental invasion. How polite!

WHOOPS, SORRY!

I'M EGGS-HAUSTED!!

In 2008, a team representing Sealand won the world egg-throwing championship!

**Proud land**

Other countries don't recognise Sealand as a real nation. But that hasn't stopped it from producing its own flag, stamps and coins. For a small fee, you can even become a Lord or Baron of Sealand.

WANT MORE?

Singer Ed Sheeran is a Baron of Sealand ✩ www.sealandgov.org/anouncements

# THE FOOD, THE BAD AND THE UGLY

Europe's a very civilised place, but that doesn't mean it can't get down and dirty when it comes to gruesome grub. Some strong-stomached Europeans swear by these delicacies, which would make a menacing menu if all served together.

**Pongy shark meat**

Never eat a freshly caught Greenland shark – it's poisonous! Icelanders get rid of the poison by gutting the shark then burying the body. Heavy stones placed on top squeeze the juices from the meat, which slowly rots for 2-3 months. The result? Hákarl – a tough, pinky-white meat which reeks of household bleach!

HMMMM... FEELING PECKISH?

## WASTE NOT, WANT NOT

Meat's on the menu a lot in Europe, and few parts of an animal are wasted. In Iceland, the testicles of male sheep are boiled and then preserved in acid to make a strong-tasting dish. Minced-up sheep's heart, liver and lungs (offal) are stuffed into a sheep's stomach (or large sausage skin) to make a haggis – the national dish of Scotland.

Haggis, mash and turnips

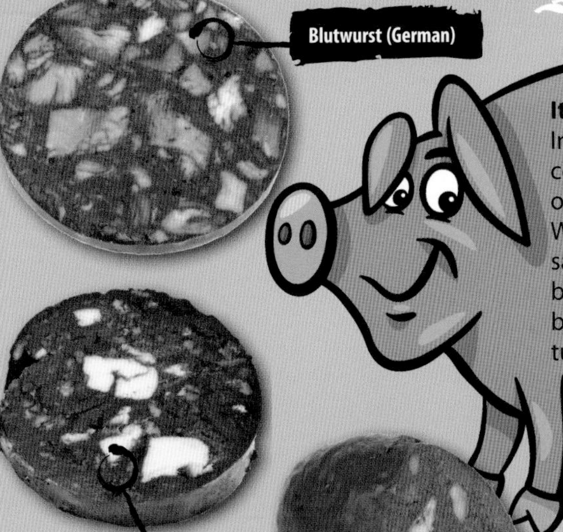


**It's in the blood**
In Germany it's usually served cold and sliced. In England it's often fried and eaten hot. What is it? The answer is sausage made mostly from the blood of pigs which has been left to congeal – turn from liquid to solid.

In some parts of Germany hot *blutwurst* served with potatoes is nicknamed *Tote Oma*, meaning 'Dead Grandma'!

WHEEEE...!

**Gooey maggot cheese**
Casu Marzu is illegal to make but some sneaky Sardinians still do. This stinky sheep's milk cheese is left outside so cheese flies *(Piophila casei)* can lay their eggs in it. The eggs hatch into maggots which wriggle through the cheese creating mushy goo. The cheese is eaten with the live maggots still inside.

Shut your eyes when you take a bite. The maggots can leap up to 15cm (6in) off the cheese!

WANT MORE?

In 2011, Lorne Coltart hurled a haggis 66m (216ft) – that's an offally long way.

# KNIGHT TIME

For centuries until the arrival of gunpowder, guns and cannons, knights were the top dogs in medieval Europe. These armoured men on horseback wowed women and awed men. Tournaments, where they displayed their skills, became colourful, exciting spectacles with battling by day and banqueting by night.

A jousting tournament on London Bridge, UK, watched by Richard II.

**The Tourney**

Tournaments began as good practice for battle but grew to provide other benefits. For lesser-known knights, they offered the chance of glory, building a reputation and being hired by a lord or king watching the spectacle.

I CAN'T SEE A THING IN HERE!

## THUNDERING HOOVES

In a joust, the knights would charge at one another down a course 100–300m (328–984ft) long. They used a long wooden pole, called a lance, to try to unseat their opponent. It took great skill to gallop at speed while holding a shield and lance.

COMING TO GET YOU, READY OR NOT!

**Bad luck**

King Henry II of France was killed in a 1559 jousting tournament when nobleman Gabriel de Montgomery's lance pierced the visor of his helmet.

GADZOOKS!

A melee

**Fearsome free-for-all**
The centrepiece of early tournaments was called a melee. This was a close-combat battle between knights on foot. Sometimes they were armed with wooden or blunted weapons. Judges would declare who won, whilst servants would carry away the dead and injured. They were kept very busy!

## WANNABE KNIGHT'S CHECKLIST

- ❑ Be born of noble blood (few peasants became knights).
- ❑ Leave home at 7 or 8 to live with a relative as a page (servant).
- ❑ Train hard to become strong and a good horserider.
- ❑ At 14–16, become a squire – a knight's apprentice.
- ❑ Work all hours to feed your knight and keep his armour clean.
- ❑ Learn to sharpen and handle weapons.
- ❑ At 20 or 21, convince a lord to dub you a knight.

Protective metal gauntlets and helmet

**Knight in shining armour**
Knights originally wore suits of chain mail, made of up to 100,000 small, interlocking metal rings. By the 1400s, suits of heavy metal plate armour were usually worn. They weighed around 25kg (55lb). For jousting, the armour could weigh almost double that. Suits were reinforced on the side nearest their opponents – usually the left.

Jousts and tournaments ✯ www.medievaleurope.mrdonn.org/jousts.html

# EAR WE GOGH

You can view over 200 paintings by Vincent van Gogh (1853–90) in Amsterdam, and hundreds more in museums and galleries in France, Germany and other European cities. Yet this amazing Dutch artist, who left behind more than 2000 pieces of art, only painted for ten years. How did he manage such a feat, and why did he cut off his ear?

Van Gogh

This is one of 37 of Van Gogh's self-portraits.

**Art life**
Van Gogh was seriously bitten by the painting bug in his late twenties. He painted for days at a time, without food or sleep, until he was totally exhausted.

*Early paintings, such as 'The Potato Eaters', were dark and gloomy. But a move to Paris, in 1886, saw van Gogh's art lighten up.*

**Thick and fast**
In Paris, van Gogh began piling on the bright colours and painting in quick, bold strokes. He was inspired by colourful Japanese art and the works of Impressionist painters.

SOLD
400 francs

CAN WE MOVE YET?

WE'VE BEEN POSING FOR HOURS!

**On sale**
Van Gogh sold just one painting whilst alive. Called *The Red Vineyard,* it went for 400 French francs (about £65 at the time). Since his death, six of his paintings have sold for more than £32 million (US$50 million) each!

## EAR FOR YOU

Van Gogh suffered from severe depression. Just before Christmas, in 1888, he sliced off part of his left ear while arguing with Paul Gauguin, another famous painter. Van Gogh then gave the chunk of ear to a lady he liked!

**A good deal**
The *Portrait of Dr Gachet* was first sold in 1897 for 300 French francs (around £42 at the time). It would change hands several times before being sold in 1990 for a staggering £82.5 million (US$128 million).

## NICKED!

More than 20 of Van Gogh's paintings have been stolen from galleries and museums. In 1975, *Breton Women* was taken and recovered twice in the space of four months from the Milan Municipal Museum in Italy.

**In 1888, he completed one painting in a single hour. Go, Van Gogh!**

# EUROVISION

In the 1950s, a European TV boss liked the idea of a friendly singing competition between nations. Just seven countries took part in the first contest in 1956, won by Switzerland. It's been held every year since. The 2013 edition held in Malmö, Sweden, welcomed singers and bands from 39 European countries in a massive live event watched by around 125 million viewers Europe-wide.

YOU SHOULD SEE MY REAL FACE!

**Famous names**
Some well-known acts have taken part in Eurovision including Cliff Richard, Katrina and the Waves and Celine Dion. In 1974, ABBA triumphed for Sweden with their song *Waterloo,* which helped to launch their worldwide pop career.

Most songs that do well at Eurovision are pop or dance tracks. But in 2006, Finnish heavy rockers Lordi won with *Hard Rock Hallelujah*. With fireworks and scary masks, the act was Finland's first-ever victory.

**Scoring points**
Each country awards points from 1 to 12 to their favourite 12 entries. Many nations are guilty of block voting – awarding high points to their neighbours. Greece and Cyprus, for example, regularly exchange high marks, as do the UK and Ireland and the former eastern bloc nations Belarus, Ukraine and Poland.

**Golden oldies**
Age is no obstacle to entering Eurovision. In 2012, the Buranovo Grannies of Russia came second, beating younger acts such as Irish pop duo Jedward!

OH NO, WE'VE BEEN FOILED AGAIN...

Jedward

To celebrate their win, Lordi held a free concert in Helsinki, Finland. 90,000 people showed up!

**Winners and losers**
Loreen won Sweden's fifth Eurovision in 2012, one of 27 nations to have succeeded. The UK has finished second the most often – a whopping 15 times. Malta, who have finished second twice and third twice, are the unluckiest nearly-rans. When it comes to losing, Norway are champs, finishing last ten times.

Loreen

**MOST SUCCESSFUL**
Ireland: 7 wins
France: 5 wins
Luxembourg: 5 wins
Sweden: 5 wins
UK: 5 wins
Netherlands: 4 wins

WANT MORE?

**Since 1975, 16 entries have received zero points in the competition. Oh dear.**

# EGGHEADS OF EUROPE

Europe has been home to some seriously big brains over the centuries. Many of these scientists have transformed how we see the world. Here, we meet six top scientists, discover what made them famous and reveal a quirkier side to their lives...

## ARCHIMEDES

**Greece (287–212BC)**

One of the first scientists to use maths to explain physical objects and movement. Explained why things float, how levers work and invented a water pump.

- His shout of 'Eureka' on discovering a scientific principle is the motto of California, USA.
- Said to have designed a death ray – it focused the Sun's rays to fry enemy soldiers!

## ISAAC NEWTON

**England (1642–1727)**

Discovered the principles of gravity, produced the three laws of motion that explain how objects move, and built the first reflecting telescope.

- Disguised himself to work undercover on the streets of London, catching fake money-makers.
- Fascinated by alchemy (turning other metals into gold).

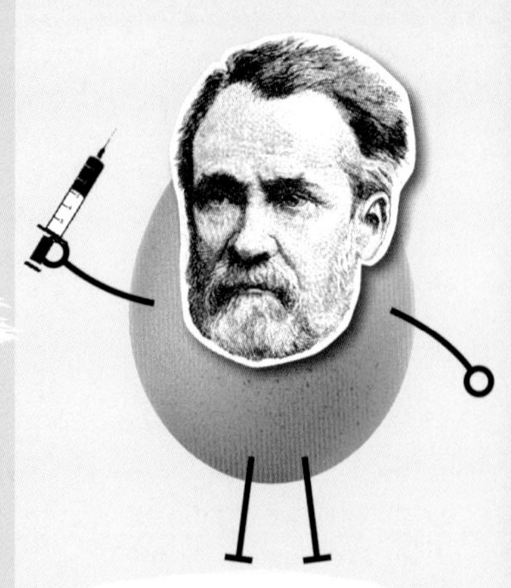

## LOUIS PASTEUR

**France (1822–85)**

Proved that most infectious diseases were caused by microorganisms. Developed ways to stop food from spoiling. Created vaccines against deadly diseases.

- Best subject at school was drawing.
- Investigating rabies, risked his life by taking samples of saliva from the mouths of raging dogs.

## NIKOLA TESLA

**Serbia (1856–1943)**

Pioneered alternating current (AC) electricity, the type used in most homes today. Transmitted electricity wirelessly, and invented the first radio-controlled model.

- Lived last ten years of his life in a New York hotel, where he fed pigeons.
- Hated shaking hands or touching hair.
- Only stayed in hotel rooms with numbers divisible by three.

## MARIE CURIE

**Poland (1867–1934)**

Investigated radioactivity and discovered, with her husband Pierre, the chemical elements radium and polonium. A pioneer in using X-rays and radiation in medicine.

- First woman to win a Nobel Prize.
- Her notebooks are still too radioactive to handle safely.
- Drove ambulances in World War I.

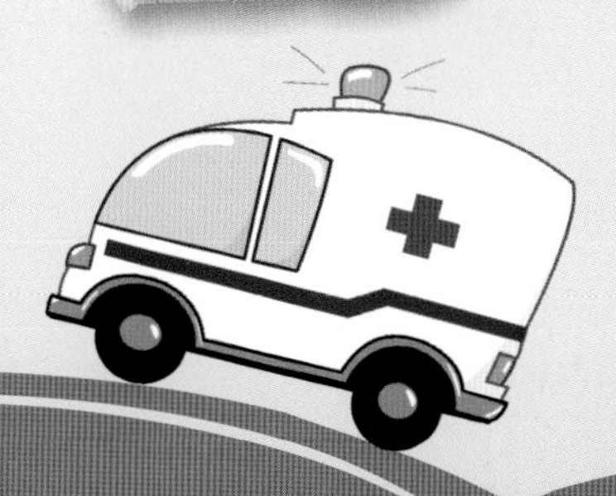

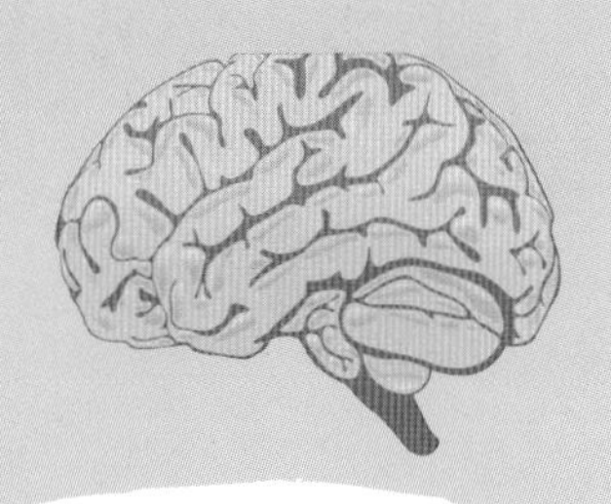

## ALBERT EINSTEIN

**Germany (1879–1955)**

Huge-brained physicist. His theories changed how people look at space, energy and matter. He explained how light works and how energy and mass (the amount of something) are related.

- After he died, his brain was removed from his body and pickled in a jar.
- Hated wearing socks and rarely did.

WANT MORE?

More about the world's best scientists ✯ www.famousscientists.org

# FUN IN FINLAND

With around 200,000 lakes, Finland is a country of great beauty. Many Finns own a lakeside holiday home, allowing them to enjoy the countryside. But it's not all peace and quiet, as wannabee world champions give it their all – rocking out to seriously loud soundtracks, ploughing through water carrying their wives or tossing their mobile phone as far as they can!

WISH YOU HADN'T EATEN THOSE BEANS!

**To have and to hold**

The World Wife Carrying Championships have been held in Sonkajärvi since 1992. Racers carry a lady on their backs around a 253.5m-long course (832ft). It has two barriers to clamber over and a large water jump to wade through. Crashes and falls occur so the wives wear helmets. Couples are timed and the fastest wins!

**Fast and furious**

By day, Taisto Miettinen is an ever-so-serious Finnish lawyer, but after work he trains to stay fit, fast and strong, and with great results. Taisto won four World Wife Carrying Championships in a row between 2009 and 2012.

## WIVES RULE!

1. The wife you carry can be yours or someone else's.
2. Wives must weigh at least 49kg (108lb).
3. If too light, the wife must wear a backpack loaded with weights.
4. The wife must be at least 17 years of age.

## CHUGGA-CHUGGA-KERRRRUNNNGG!

Once a year, the Finnish town of Oulu really rocks to the Air Guitar World Championships. Contestants from all over the world mime playing a guitar in front of a crowd of thousands. Judges mark their performance on style, accuracy and timing with the music. Champions have come from New Zealand, Japan and the United States.

WHADDAYA MEAN, YOU DON'T LIKE MY SUIT?!

**Brrring, brrring fling**
Bet you've wanted to chuck your clunky mobile at some point or another? Well, at Savonlinna, you can, and you might even become world champion doing so. There's a junior competition for phone throwers under 12, too.

**At the weigh-in**
Any mobile phone weighing at least 220g (8oz) is suitable for the competition – but not your parents' latest device, eh? All the broken parts are scooped up afterwards and recycled.

In 2012, Ere Karjalainen from Finland threw his phone 101.46m (333ft), a new world record.

= 20m (66ft)

WANT MORE?

Germany's Aline Westphal became the first female air guitar world champion in 2011.

# THE BONE SCULPTOR

Just outside the small Czech town of Kutná Hora, 80km (50mi) east of the capital, Prague, lies Sedlec. A monastery was built in Sedlec 900 years ago, and today it is home to the Cemetery Church of All Saints. Nothing remarkable you might think – until you step inside...

Sedlec Ossuary's masterpiece is this incredible chandelier. It's made out of at least one of each of the 206 different bones that make up the human body.

**Dishing the dirt**

It all started when the head of the monastery, Abbot Jindřich, visited the Middle East in 1278. He returned with soil from the supposed burial site of Jesus Christ and sprinkled it over the cemetery. As word spread, more and more people wanted their loved ones to be buried in the holy soil of Sedlec.

Sedlec Ossuary contains the bones of more than 40,000 skeletons.

THESE BONE-ATIONS ARE VERY NICE . . .

BUT I HAVEN'T GOT ANY BODY TO SPEND THEM ON!

**A grave matter**

The number of bodies buried at Sedlec soared during the Black Death (*see* p86). Soon, there were too many for the cemetery, so a chapel was built for the surplus skeletons. Old graves were also dug up and the bones taken inside. Such stores are called ossuaries.

## SKELETON ARTIST

The bones kept piling up until 1870 when the local Schwarzenberg family bought the chapel. They employed František Rint, a carpenter and woodcarver, to organise all the bones in the chapel. It's fair to say that Rint outdid himself!

*Rint arranged the bones to form patterns on the walls and sculptures around the chapel. He hung garlands of leg bones and skulls from the ceiling.*

**Coat of bones**
František Rint was no fool. He sucked up to his employers big time with this elaborate bony interpretation of the Schwarzenberg family coat of arms.

**Bones not alone**
One of Europe's biggest ossuaries is in Brno, also in the Czech Republic. It holds around 50,000 skeletons and was only rediscovered in 2001 during building work. Imagine the surprise!

WANT MORE?

See Brno ossuary ✩ www.atlasobscura.com/places/ brno-ossuary

During the 17th century, there were 10,000 gondolas on Venice's canals.

# SO YOU WANT TO BE A GONDOLIER?

The Italian city of Venice is made up of over 100 islands criss-crossed by a network of 177 canals and more than 400 bridges. Fancy a life as a gondolier, working in the open air, meeting people and seeing the sites as you transport tourists through the scenic canals? Reckon it would be a doddle to get into? Think it would take next-to-no training? WRONG!

## TOP GEAR: *GONDOLA*

LENGTH: 10.9m (35.8ft)
WIDTH: 1.42m (4.7ft)
WEIGHT (EMPTY): 700kg (1543lb)
ENGINE: 1 oar power
TOP SPEED: about 4km/h (2.5mph)
0-60: Are you kidding?
NUMBER OF PARTS: 280
MATERIAL: Eight types of wood: lime, larch, oak, fir, cherry, walnut, elm and mahogany.

**Jobs for the boys... until now**
For over 900 years, gondoliering was only for men. Women had tried and failed the exam until 24-year-old Giorgia Boscolo became the first gondoliera in 2010.

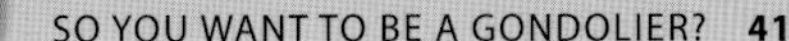

**Keep it in the family**
Today, there are only 425 gondolas. All are piloted by licenced members of the 1000-year-old Gondolier's Guild. Only a few new licences are awarded each year, mostly to other family members.

**Heavy metal**
*Il Ferro*, 'the steel', is a large ornament on the front of a gondola which balances the weight of the back of the boat. The six metal blades symbolise the six historical districts of Venice.

**Gone gondoliering**
You're looking at serious training time to become a gondolier – over 400 hours! Then, there's a tough exam that'll test your strength, boat handling and navigation skills. Gondoliers must know every city site and route. Many fail the test.

Regular gondolas in Venice are painted black, but at festival time blinged-up larger versions take to the canals.

## OAR AND PEACE

Modern gondolas are open to the weather. They weigh a tonne when full of passengers, and are propelled by a single oar. The oar acts as a motor and brakes. It also steers the gondola down crowded canals and during super-tight turns.

WANT MORE?

Early gondola (above) had closed cabins for secret meetings, romance and kidnappings!

A Spartan army charges into battle.

# A SPARTAN LIFE

Growing up as a boy in the ancient Greek city-state of Sparta 2500 years ago was no picnic. Many Greek states devoted themselves to learning and the arts. Sparta was different. From the 6th century BC onwards, it was warlike and kept a strong army at the ready all the time. So if you think your routine of homework and chores is tough, check out life as a Spartan schoolboy.

**Soldier school**
As soon as Spartan boys reached seven, they left their families and went to live in army barracks. They slept on the floor and had just one cloak per year to wear. To toughen them up, the boys were underfed, beaten regularly and made to walk barefoot.

## THE 300

The Spartan army's most famous battle was actually a defeat in 480 BC. Led by King Leonidas, just 300 Spartans and some 1100 other Greek soldiers defended Thermopylae against Emperor Xerxes' vast Persian army of more than 100,000. Leonidas' brave lot held out for three days.

Spartan soldiers

**Deadly cheese**
Boys trained in all the arts of fighting and survival. There were no maths exams to sweat over, but there was a brutal cheese-stealing contest every year. Competitors tried to snatch cheese from an altar whilst their classmates flogged them with leather whips. A 'fail' in this test often meant boys died from their wounds.

**Seven to sixty**
All this hard living and training turned boys into super strong warriors. At age 20, they became soldiers of the Spartan army until retiring at 60 – if they lived that long! No worries if they didn't, as there were always new kids on the block waiting to replace them.

metal helmet topped with horse hair

large spear

dagger-shaped sword

round shield made of bronze or wood

A Spartan warrior ready for combat

Sparta was no place for weaklings. Tiny or feeble baby boys were often left to die on Mount Taygetos.

WANT MORE?

Black broth (pork cooked in pig's blood) was a typical Spartan soldier's dinner. Yuk!

# TOY STORY

What toy is there more than 62 of for every man, woman and child on the planet? If you answered LEGO® bricks, you'd be right! They were the invention of Ole Kirk Christiansen, a carpenter from Billund in Denmark, and his son Godtfred. Christiansen started out making deadly dull wooden ladders and ironing boards. When sales fell during the 1930s, he had to think of something more fun for people to buy.

PLASTIC BRICKS, OLE? YOU'RE QUACKERS!

The world's tallest LEGO tower of 2011 was built in Paris, France.

**Name of the game**
Ole Christiansen made a toy wooden duck for his sons and, seeing how much they liked it, began producing wooden toys to sell to others. In 1934, he named his business after the Danish words for 'play well' – Leg Godt – shortened to LEGO. In a handy coincidence, it turned out that LEGO means 'I put together' in Latin.

**Father and son of LEGO**
Godtfred Christiansen was only four when he and his brother Karl burnt down their father's house and workshop whilst playing with wood shavings. Godtfred owed his father big time! He found a way to repay him in the early 1950s. Together with his dad they dreamt up the idea of toys made of interlocking plastic bricks.

COULD SOMEONE PLEASE GET THIS CAT OFF MY BACK?!

There are 915 million different ways you can combine six eight-studded LEGO bricks.

## PARK LIFE

In 1968, Godtfred opened the first LEGOLAND theme park next to the company's factories in Billund. Over 50 million bricks were used to build its exhibits, which are seen by 1.6 million people every year. Five more parks have since opened – in England, Germany and Malaysia, and two in the USA.

**Grown-up LEGO**

Adult Fans of LEGO (AFOL) exist all over the world. Some are record breakers. The world record for the tallest LEGO tower has changed hands over 30 times since 1988. In 2012, a 32.5m-high tower (106.6ft) made of 500,000 bricks went up in the Czech city of Prague to become the tallest so far.

**Big brick numbers**

**x5**

All the LEGO bricks sold in a year, laid end to end, would circle the Earth over five times.

**19 billion**

19 billion LEGO bricks and other parts are produced every year at the factories in Billund – that's 36,000 pieces every minute.

**40 billion**

40,000,000,000 LEGO bricks would be needed, stacked on top of each other, to reach the Moon from Earth. Far out!

See other LEGO record breakers ✯ www.recordholders.org/en/list/lego.html

# SARAJEVO SUN

## THE SHOTS THAT SHOOK THE WORLD

In 1914, there was great unrest in Europe. Countries had built up their armed forces as they jostled for power. Smaller regions wanted freedom from larger countries or empires. The whole continent was a time bomb waiting to explode.

THE ARCHDUKE AND HIS WIFE, SOPHIE, ARRIVE AT SARAJEVO STATION.

**Amateur assassin**

A secret group called Black Hand recruited student Gavrilo Princip. His job was to kill Austro-Hungarian heir to the throne, Archduke Franz Ferdinand, during a visit to Sarajevo in Serbia in 1914.

The Black Hand movement wanted freedom from the Austro-Hungarian empire.

### BUMBLING KILLERS!

Gavrilo Princip was not the only assassin. There were another six members of the Black Hand. Each had grenades or bombs, a gun and a cyanide pill to commit suicide with after the attack.

- The first assassin lost his nerve and let the Archduke's car go past.
- The second lobbed his grenade but it bounced off the car and rolled under a vehicle behind, injuring those inside.
- The Archduke's car sped off and the other assassins, including Princip, gave up and trudged off.

MAYHEM ON FRANZ JOSEPH STREET AS PRINCIP SHOOTS. . .

## WRONG WAY

Archduke Ferdinand was outraged at the bungled attack, but later went to visit those who had been injured. A general decided the car should take a different route but no one told the driver! As he turned into Franz Joseph Street he was ordered to reverse.

## BANG, BANG

Princip was standing outside a shop in Franz Joseph Street. He was surprised to see the Archduke's car right in front of him. As the driver tried to reverse, the car's engine stalled. Princip fired two shots from his gun, killing the Archduke and his wife.

### Gavrilo's fate

Princip turned his gun on himself, but was wrestled to the ground. Although charged with double murder, he was too young for the death penalty. He was sent to prison instead, where he died of tuberculosis in 1918.

## WORLD AT WAR

Austro-Hungary was outraged and declared war on Serbia on 28 July 1914. The major nations of Europe took sides. Germany and the Ottoman Empire supported Austro-Hungary. Russia, Britain and France all entered the war on the side of Serbia. World War I (1914–18) became the largest and most destructive war the world had ever seen.

WANT MORE?

Read all about it ☆ www.firstworldwar.com/source/harrachmemoir.htm

**All you can eat**
Lotito started munching serious metal objects – from bicycles to beds – in his teens. He swallowed small pieces washed down with mineral oil and lots of water. Doctors found he had a stomach lining twice as thick as normal.

# IN AND OUT

Humans need a little iron in their diet, but one man took it to extremes. Born in Grenoble, France, Michel Lotito (1950–2007) had a strange urge to eat things made of metal, glass and rubber. It began when his parents caught him gnawing their old television set. His nickname was Monsieur Mangetout (Mr Eats All).

By 1997, Monsieur Mangetout had chomped more than 8 tonnes (9 tons) of metal!

It was the first time a coffin ended up inside a man instead of the man ending up inside a coffin!

On Monsieur Mangetout's
MENU

18 bicycles
15 supermarket trolleys
7 TV sets
6 chandeliers
2 beds
1 pair of skis
1 coffin

**In-flight dining**
Like your food plain? Well, Lotito liked planes as food! His greatest extreme eating act took two years (1979–80). He scoffed an entire Cessna 150 light aircraft – propeller, wings and all.

## WINDY CITY

Another unique Frenchman was Joseph Pujol (1857–1945). He could suck in and blow out air through his bottom at will. Paris became the windy city during the 1890s when Pujol starred at the famous Moulin Rouge Theatre.

For a time, Pujol was the highest-paid entertainer in France, earning around the wages of 250 school teachers at once.

**Candles in the wind**
Pujol used his unusual skill to imitate musical instruments and farm animals. He could play tunes, including the French national anthem, and could blow out candles from a distance. King Leopold II of Belgium and Prince Edward of Wales were amongst his many fans.

WANT MORE?
Watch Michel munch metal ✯ www.youtube.com/watch?v=h6PI2-lx12A

# THE EMPIRE STRIKES BACK

*Sultan Mehmed II's army surrounds Constantinople, 1453.*

Europe has had more than its fair share of grand empires. But from the 15th century onwards, a new power really put the wind up the rest of Europe. The Ottoman, or Turkish, Empire captured Constantinople in 1453. They renamed it Istanbul and made it the centre of an empire that grew fast and furious. Ruthlessness and brutality were two of many reasons for the Empire's success.

**One king to rule all**

The Ottoman Empire concentrated power in one ruler, the Sultan, so decisions could be made fast. On coming to power, some sultans had their brothers murdered so they couldn't plot and overthrow them.

CAN'T THINK WHY I'VE GOT A HEADACHE!

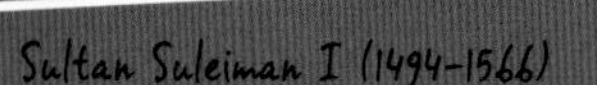


**Fighting forces**

Ottoman armies were fierce and brave in battle. Under skilled generals, such as Sultans Mehmed II and Suleiman I, they conquered much of Eastern Europe. Their elite troops, called Janissaries, were well-drilled, well-paid and lived together as a tight-knit unit.

A Janissary

## YOU'RE FIRED!

Ottoman armies combined brutal hand-to-hand fighting methods with more modern guns and cannons. The Great Turkish Bombard was a huge cannon which could fire a giant cannonball as far as 3km (2mi). This powerful weapon helped destroy the walls of Constantinople.

Topkapi Palace

**Making an example**

From the moment you reached the Sultan's home in Istanbul, you knew he meant business. Displayed outside the Imperial Gate of Topkapi Palace were the heads of freshly executed criminals. Inside the palace, the stuffed heads of nobles who'd angered the Sultan were placed on marble pillars, called example stones.

The tughra was the official signature or seal of a sultan.

Tughra used as sultan's signature on official documents

**Soft in the head**

The heads of executed major nobles were cut off and stuffed with soft cotton. Those of less important nobles were stuffed with straw.

I'M FEELNG A BIT FUZZY-HEADED!

**It wasn't all war, war, war**

Some sultans proved skilled at non-military matters, creating schools and boosting trade. Suleiman I, for example, revamped Istanbul by building 26 libraries, 17 hospitals and 132 mosques. He encouraged many arts including calligraphy.

**During Sultan Selim I's eight-year rule, 30,000 people were executed.**

# FOOTBALL CRAZEEEE!

Europeans are mad about football. In fact it's the continent's favourite sport. Europe is home to many of the world's greatest football clubs, from Bayern Munich, Germany, to Manchester United, UK. It's packed with clubs, big and small, who are fiercely competitive. When they play each other, it's derby day. Watch the sparks fly!

## SUPER STADIA

For a derby match to really buzz you need a great stadium packed with fans. The biggest club stadium in Europe is Barcelona's Camp Nou ground in Spain, which holds over 98,000 spectators.

German football clubs, such as Schalke and Borussia Dortmund, pack out their games. The country's top 36 clubs sold 18.8 million tickets in the 2011/12 season.

**Turkish delight**

Turkey is home to a fearsome derby between Fenerbahçe and Galatasaray. Fenerbahçe have won more games, but Galatasaray supporters still brag about their biggest-ever win of 7–0 in 1911. This is even more impressive given that Galatasaray only had seven players.

Fenerbahçe fans fly the flag outside their home stadium in Istanbul.

COME ON, WHERE ARE YOU?

OVER HERE, BEHIND THE GOAL.

The biggest thrashing ever in an El Clásico derby saw Real Madrid beat Barcelona 11-1 in 1943.

Lionel Messi scored 73 goals in the 2011/12 season – a European record.

GO AND PLAY ON THE WING!

Cristiano Ronaldo

Lionel Messi

**Mascot madness**
Many European footie clubs have a cuddly chum called a mascot to greet younger fans. Occasionally, the mascots go derby day crazy and push or even fight their opponent.

## REIGN IN SPAIN

The big El Clásico derby in Spain is between the country's two most successful teams – Real Madrid and Barcelona. These teams are packed with the greatest footballers around. Real have Cristiano Ronaldo – the world's highest-paid footballer at about £27.5 million (US$42 million) per year. Barcelona have Lionel Messi – the world's best player.

WANT MORE?

Learn about football derbies all over Europe ✮ www.footballderbies.com

# EXTINCT IN EUROPE



Europe may have less extreme wildlife than other continents, but it's still home to monkeys (barbary macaques in Gibraltar), wild boar, grey wolves and more than 30 species of bat. Sadly, some of its more exotic creatures have died out during past centuries. These include the great auk, a hefty seabird once found on islands throughout northernmost Europe.

**Sitting ducks**

Great auks were hunted for thousands of years. Originally, they were snared for their meat and eggs. But from the 15th to 17th centuries their feathers became highly prized for stuffing pillows. Brilliant underwater, the birds were clumsy on land and easy to catch.

FOR SALE
£300

In the 19th century, you could buy a small house in Europe for the price of a 12cm-long great auk's egg (5in) - £300 (US$458).

The more great auk numbers plummeted, the more they were hunted. Europe's museums were booming and all wanted auks (dead or alive) for their displays. The last known pair of birds were killed by Icelandic fishermen in 1844.

**Auks' end**
The last great auk in Britain was killed in 1840 by three sailors who feared it was a witch. Doh!

**Recently departed**
Other large European animals have also become extinct since the great auk. These include the Caspian tiger, which inhabited Georgia, Turkey and Russia until the mid-20th century. The last tarpan died in Poland, 1879. The pied raven of the Faroe Islands died out in 1948. And the last Pyrenean ibex died in 2000.

Tarpan

Pyrenean ibex

I FEEL A HEADACHE COMING ON...

## EXOTIC EXTINCTIONS

European lions once roamed Greece and the Balkans. Parts of Europe were also home to European cheetahs, cave hyenas, and Eurasian aurochs (giant wild cattle). There were also Irish elks with 4m-wide antlers (13ft).

WHO ARE YOU CALLING SHORTY?

Irish elk

Cave hyena skull

**Tiny tusks**
Cyprus was once home to its own species of pygmy hippos and dwarf elephants. These stunted mammals stood no taller than 90cm (35in). Ah, bless.

Pygmy hippo

WANT MORE?

**Declared extinct in 1962, Bavarian pine voles were rediscovered in Austria in 2000.**

# PETER'S PLACE



In 2012, St Petersburg's population passed five million. Russia's second-largest city is also its most westernised, and for that one can thank (or blame) their former ruler, Tsar Peter I (1672–1725), or Peter the Great. Fascinated by ships as a child, Peter knew his country needed sea ports in the Baltic to trade with other nations. He went to war with Sweden to capture new territory.



**On tour**

In 1697, Peter left Russia and toured Europe, learning about how other countries were run. He worked as an ordinary labourer in the Dutch shipyards. Peter returned a big fan of western ways. He was determined to modernise Russia.

Monument of Peter the Great in Moscow, Russia

Peter dressed as a carpenter on his European tour

On tour Peter disguised himself as a ship's carpenter called Peter Mikhailov. He fooled no one. At 2.04m (6.7ft), he was one of Europe's tallest men and towered over almost everyone he met.

## WAR AND PETE

St Petersburg was founded in 1703 when Peter's armies grabbed the Neva River delta, an area of swampy land and islands in the Gulf of Finland. There, they built the Peter and Paul Fortress (above). The first building erected was a three-roomed wooden cabin for Peter. It was knocked up in just three days and still stands today.

**Tsar quality**
Peter moved his capital from Moscow to his new city in St Petersburg in 1712. It was one of many sweeping changes he introduced. The Tsar formed Russia's navy and built the country's first modern hospitals. He encouraged mining, industry and trade. He discouraged forced marriage and old ways of living.

One of the prisoners in the Peter and Paul Fortress was Peter's own son, Alexei. He was tortured and died there in 1718.

BUT I CAN AFFORD TO PAY FOR IT!

**Off with their beards**
Under Peter, old fashions and beards were out. He personally and brutally cut off nobles' beards and slashed their traditional clothes. Anyone desperate to keep their beard had to pay a massive tax for the privilege.

WANT MORE?

**Prankster Peter built trick fountains at his palace, Peterhof, to soak nobles to the skin.**

Kings and queens once ruled most of Europe but how many of those countries have reigning royalty today? One? Two? The answer is ten. Can you name them all?* Now, if you think kings and queens are dusty old figures you only read about in history books, you may be in for a surprise as you check out these fun-loving royals.

# KINGS AND QUEENS OF EUROPE

OUT WITH THE OLD THRONE!

**King Willem-Alexander**
Meet brand new Dutch monarch Willem-Alexander. He took charge in 2013 after his mother, Queen Beatrix stepped down. The new king's an all-action kind of guy, having run the New York marathon, competed in an ice skating marathon and piloted a jet aircraft.

*The king takes part in a toilet-throwing competition on Queen's Day in the Netherlands*

King Willem-Alexander

**Queen Margrethe II**
Margrethe II is the first queen of Denmark to rule by herself. This talented queen's paintings have appeared in many major European exhibitions and she illustrated the Danish edition of *The Lord of the Rings*. She's also a fashion designer whose costumes have appeared in ballets and in movies.

Queen Margrethe II

***Ten Thrones:** Belgium, Britain, Denmark, the Netherlands, Norway, Spain, Sweden, Liechtenstein, Monaco and Luxembourg.

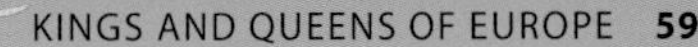


**Queen Elizabeth II**
The 40th British monarch since William the Conqueror in 1066, Queen Elizabeth II has reigned for over 60 years. But far from being locked in the past, the Queen launched her own website in 1997 and sent her first email in 1976 – long before you did!

## QUEEN ELIZABETH II BY NUMBERS

Ships launched:
**21**

Letters received:
**3.5 million**

THE QUEEN
Buckingham Palace
London

Official overseas visits made:
**over 250**

Telegrams to people celebrating 100th birthdays:
**175,000**

Christmas puddings given to staff:
**90,000**

THE KING'S HERE... GULP!

**King Juan Carlos**
Fond of taking anonymous cross-country motorbike rides, the king speaks five languages of Spain speaks five languages and has hunted bears (which upsets some of his subjects). Juan Carlos also competed at the 1972 Olympic games, sailing yachts.

Monaco's reigning monarch, Prince Albert II, competed at five Winter Olympics in the bobsleigh.

WANT MORE?

Check out Europe's royalty ✫ www.royaltymonarchy.com/royfacts/current.html

# VIVA PASTA

If you believe the cliché of Italians loving their lasagne and linguine and slurping their spaghetti… then you'd be right! No one makes or eats more pasta than the average Italian – over 26kg (57lb) of the stuff each year. That's a good 100–150 meals worth a year and double that of any other country.

**In the distant pasta**
No one knows who actually invented pasta. But we know it was being made in China and in Arabia hundreds of years ago. It was even eaten by the Etruscans, who lived in the area that is now Italy more than 2400 years ago!

**Footing the bill**
Pasta was originally made by hand or, in Italy, by feet. The tough dough was kneaded by workers treading on it for up to a day before it was rolled out. Thankfully, Cesare Spadaccini invented a machine to replace the footwork in the 19th century.

**Simply does it**
There are more than 600 types and shapes of pasta. Some types are made fresh with egg. Others consist of flour, water and salt which is then dried for up to 50 hours.

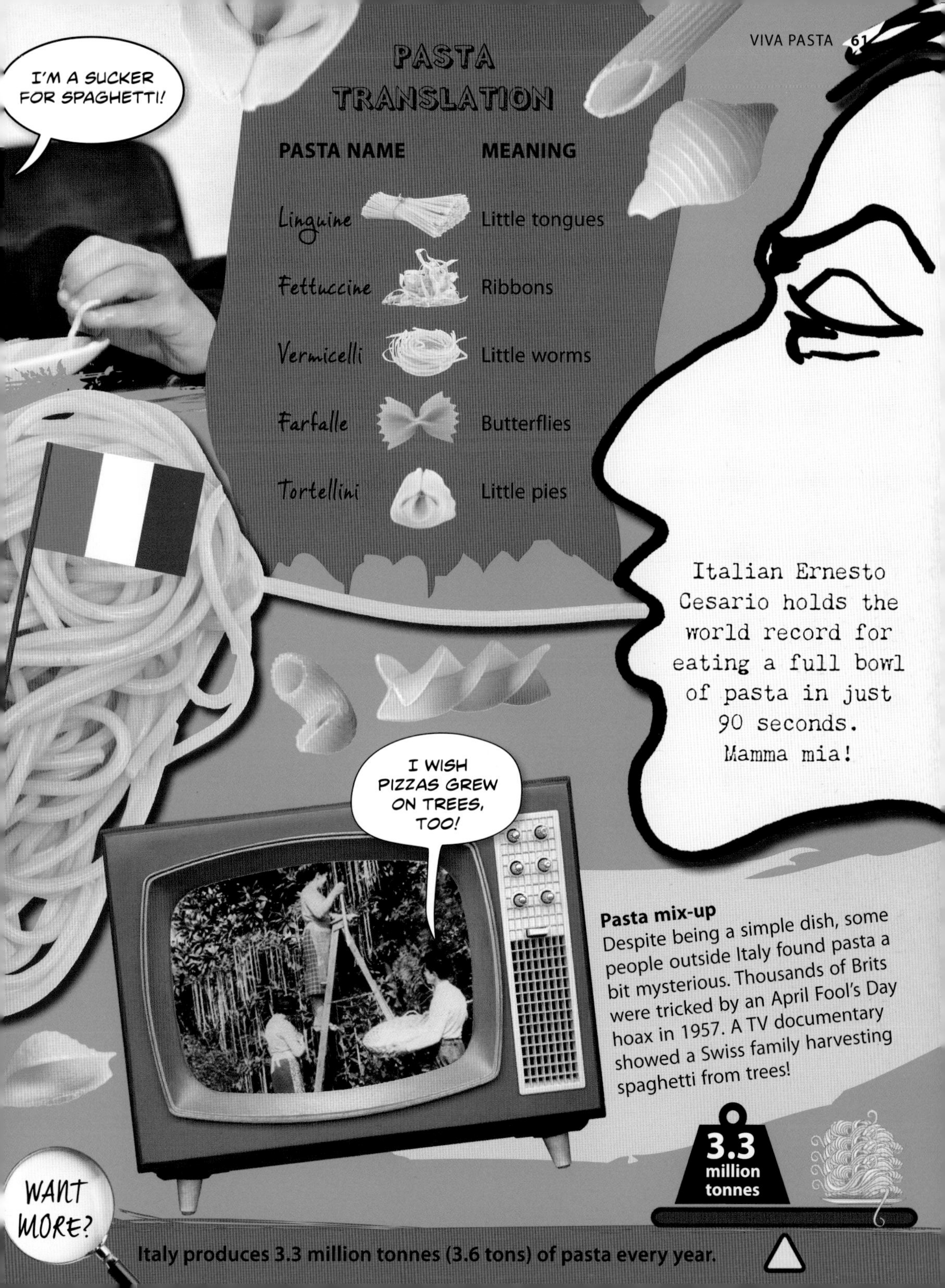


## PASTA TRANSLATION

| PASTA NAME | MEANING |
| --- | --- |
| Linguine | Little tongues |
| Fettuccine | Ribbons |
| Vermicelli | Little worms |
| Farfalle | Butterflies |
| Tortellini | Little pies |

Italian Ernesto Cesario holds the world record for eating a full bowl of pasta in just 90 seconds. Mamma mia!

**Pasta mix-up**
Despite being a simple dish, some people outside Italy found pasta a bit mysterious. Thousands of Brits were tricked by an April Fool's Day hoax in 1957. A TV documentary showed a Swiss family harvesting spaghetti from trees!

WANT MORE?

**Italy produces 3.3 million tonnes (3.6 tons) of pasta every year.**

# UNFINISHED BUSINESS

Antoni Gaudí (1852–1926) graduated from Barcelona's School of Architecture, Spain, in 1878. Its director said aloud, 'Gentlemen, we are here today in the presence of either a genius or a madman.' For much of Gaudí's life, people remained undecided.

Gaudí planned the Sagrada Familia to have 18 towering spires, the tallest rising 170m (558ft). Eight were in place by 2010.

YOU'VE GOT TO THINK BIG...

Antoni Gaudí

When complete, the church will hold up to 9000 people!

**Started small, finished BIG**
Gaudí's first job as an architect was nothing more grand than a set of lamp posts for squares in Barcelona. But he soon got bigger commissions, and in 1883 began work on his masterpiece, a giant new church in Barcelona – the Sagrada Familia.

Sagrada Familia

**Slow progress**
Gaudí was a perfectionist and took his time. He preferred making models to producing building plans and wasn't worried by delays. When he was killed by a tram in 1926, the Sagrada Familia was less than a quarter completed. Work continues to this day, with the hope that it will be completed in 2026.

OH, MY HEAD!

To see how a donkey statue would look high up on part of the church, Gaudí had a real live one lifted up by cranes working on the church.

**Antoni's antics**
Gaudí was a vegetarian, never married, was famous for his short temper and insisted on wearing shabby suits. He also preferred second-hand shoes, so he got his brother Francesc to wear in new pairs for him first.

## PARK LIFE

Barcelona's Park Güell was built between 1900 and 1916. Gaudí designed it as a city park, full of fairytale buildings and mosaic tiles.

Dragon at Park Güell

After he died, Gaudí was buried in the crypt of his unfinished church.

WANT MORE?

**The Sagrada Familia church is almost the size of a football pitch.**

Stretching across eight countries, from Slovenia to France, the Alps mountain range is packed full of peaks. Over 80 of these reach 4000m (13,123ft) or above. Today, thousands of climbers attempt to scale them for the challenge. But less than 200 years ago most peaks had yet to be climbed.

**Mont Blanc**
The tallest of the Alps, Mont Blanc, was one of the first to be conquered in 1786. The two-man team of Jacques Balmat and Michel-Gabriel Paccard didn't use ropes or ice axes. Their only climbing equipment was an alpenstock – a long wooden pole with an iron spike on one end.

Memorial plaque to Balmat and Paccard

**Drawing on experience**
Edward Whymper was a young illustrator who travelled to the Alps in 1860 to draw scenes of the mountains. He quickly fell under their spell and learned how to climb from local guides. In 1864, he was part of the first group to climb Barre des Écrins in the Alps. He was also the first to climb five other Alpine peaks in 1864 and 1865.

Edward Whymper

**The murderous Matterhorn**

Whymper's biggest mountaineering test was the mighty Matterhorn. He made eight failed attempts to climb it before he succeeded in 1865. Hours after the success came tragedy when four of his seven-man party fell to their deaths on the way down.

## A GOLDEN AGE

The mid-19th century is known as the golden age of Alpinism. It's when most of the major peaks were climbed (the last being Meije in 1877). Many of the climbers wore jackets and ties but no protective helmets. Nor did they have GPS, fleeces or other hi-tech climbing gear.

**In 2007, Slovenian Miha Valič climbed 82 Alpine peaks in just 102 days.**

Leonardo da Vinci

# THINKING MAN

You've probably got friends who are brilliant at more than one thing. Annoying, aren't they? Well imagine being Leonardo da Vinci's pal! The Renaissance (14th–17th centuries) was when Europe woke up and really started thinking about things. Leonardo da Vinci (1452–1519) was the ultimate Renaissance man. He was a thinker, painter, engineer, inventor and scientist. Oh, and he also played a mean lyre (stringed instrument).

A lyre

**Paint job**
Leo often switched from one artwork to another and left many unfinished and now lost. Some of his works that have survived include the mysterious *Mona Lisa* and the enormous 8.8m-long mural (29ft) of *The Last Supper.*


Mona Lisa

The Last Supper

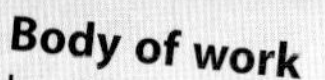

**Body of work**

Leo's interest in anatomy saw him dissect human corpses to learn the secrets inside. He filled notebook upon notebook of detailed sketches. These included his famous Vitruvian Man sketch. It shows how each part of the human body is in proportion.

*Vitruvian Man, 1490*

Leonardo was a vegetarian and often bought caged birds which he released into the wild.

x6
= your height

Measure your foot then multiply by six. The answer should be close to your height. Thanks, Leo!

*3D model of the ornithopter*

Amongst da Vinci's sketches and plans were a mechanical flying bat, called an ornithopter, and winged boots for walking on water!

*Model of the armoured boat designed by Leo*

**Ahead of his time**

Leo drew plans for devices that the world wouldn't see for centuries. His ideas included helicopters and parachutes, the bicycle, solar power, and an armoured tank that could carry eight men. Some of his inventions, such as lens grinding machines, were built and became a great success.

WANT MORE?

**Da Vinci wrote all his notes backwards, possibly to keep them secret!**

Superyacht marina in Monaco

# HOT SPOTS

You're an uber-rich celebrity with money to burn. Perhaps you'd kick back and relax on your own private island, like shipping magnate Aristotle Onassis (owner of the Greek island of Skorpios) or Portuguese footballer Cristiano Ronaldo (who owns Deserta Island near Madeira). Or, you might glide around the most luxurious hot spots seeking out the best and most expensive Europe has to offer.

**Luxury travel**
In the past you might take the luxurious Orient Express train from Paris in France to Istanbul in Turkey. But today you're just as likely to jet in to a private airstrip or sail your superyacht into an exclusive members-only marina at Monaco, Capri, Portafino, or Hvar in Croatia.

The best rooms in Hotel President Wilson in Geneva, Switzerland, can cost £42,000 (US$65,000) a night. Ouch!

## BRMMM, BRMMM

If cars are your thing, head to the French-German border. This is where Bugatti build the world's fastest and most expensive supercar – the Veyron 16.4 Super Sport. A souped-up Veyron can reach 431km/h (268mph) and could set you back £2.1 million (US$3.2 million).

## HUNGRY FOR SUCCESS

Millionaires might plump for a Seafood Treasure curry at London's Bombay Brasserie. A snip at £2000 (US$3000) per person! Or perhaps a meal at Solo Per Due – an entire restaurant in Varone, Italy, for just two dinner guests. Until it closed in 2011, Spain's El Bulli eaterie lavished guests with 30-course meals which took five hours to eat!

£2000

100

PLEASE DON'T LET ANYONE SEE ME LIKE THIS!

**Pampered pooches**

Every year fashionistas head for the catwalk shows in Milan, Paris, London and Madrid. For glittering jewels, Antwerp in Belgium's the place to go. Over 60% of the world's diamonds are traded there. A diamond dog collar could set you back £100,000 (US$155,440)!

## WHEEL OF FORTUNE

Wealthy gamblers head to Monaco to try their luck at the Monte Carlo Casino. In 1873, ten years after the casino opened, British engineer Joseph Jagger won big time. He was the first player to break the bank.

**Stinking rich**

In the past, European royals and nobles drenched themselves and their rooms in scent to mask the stench of body odour and poor sanitation. Today, Guerlain is one of France's leading perfume houses. Its special edition Idylle fragrance comes in an 18-carat-gold bottle that you have to break to open, and costs almost £30,000 (US$46,632).

DARLING, I'M WORTH IT!

WANT MORE?

In 2011, a flat in One Hyde Park in London sold for £136 million (US$207 million)!

# SPY CITY

If you were a spy in the years after World War II, Berlin was the place to be. The German city was crawling with undercover agents and informers. Berlin marked the border between a Europe divided in two. It was split into those nations in the West, allied to the United States, and those in the East, supported by the Soviet Union. Both sides in the Cold War (1945–90) tried all sorts of tricks to steal secrets from each other.

ANYONE HERE NOT A SPY?

**Split city, two countries**
After World War II, Germany was split into two countries, East and West Germany. The border between the two countries ran through the centre of Berlin. Both sides in the Cold War confronted each other head-to-head.

TOP SECRET

Tiny cameras were fitted inside ties and suit jackets to snap spies and secrets without anyone knowing.

CAN'T CATCH ME!

Markus Wolf

**The man with no face**
Top East German spymaster Markus Wolf was so shady, it took the West 25 years to snap a photograph of him. Wolf placed hundreds of spies throughout Berlin, and even inside the West German government. One of his opponents, West German spymaster Hans Joachim Tiedge, turned out to be an East German spy recruited by Wolf!

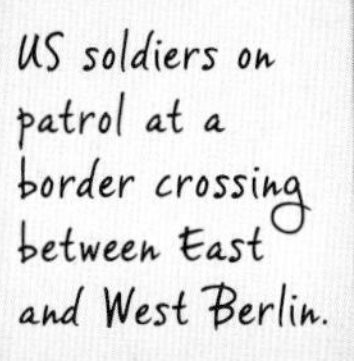

*US soldiers on patrol at a border crossing between East and West Berlin.*

**Bridge of spies**

If you were caught as a spy, death or imprisonment were likely options. Sometimes, though, the two sides would exchange captured enemy agents. Many of these spy swaps occurred on the edge of Berlin at Glienicke Bridge.

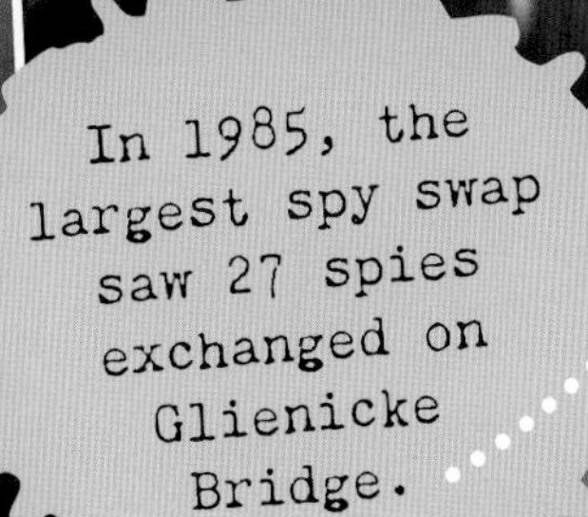


*The spy tunnel is uncovered by East Germans in 1956.*

**Going underground**

A daring mission in the 1950s saw British and American spies dig a top-secret tunnel under East Berlin so that East German phone lines could be tapped and calls listened to. The tunnel was rumbled in 1956, but not before around 440,000 phone calls had been recorded.

**450** m-long tunnel (1476ft)

**440,000** phone calls

WANT MORE?

Read about the Cold War ✰ www.ducksters.com/history/cold_war/berlin_wall.php

# SEEING STARS

During the 16th and 17th centuries, Europeans were so self-centred they thought the Sun, the planets, and the entire universe moved around Earth. Today, we know it isn't all about us. But at the time, few dared to question this view, especially as it was supported by the all-powerful Church. It took a ridiculously smart and rebellious scientist to provide the proof. His name? Galileo Galilei (1564–1642).

**Making a spectacle of yourself**
In 1609, Galileo heard about Dutch spectacle makers who fitted two lenses in a tube to view distant objects. Galileo soon whisked up his own version. It only offered three-times (3x) magnification. But he quickly developed more powerful lenses. Galileo created an 8x telescope which he showed off to the bigwigs of Venice.

Galileo's views of the moon through his telescope.

**Looking up**
By the winter of 1609, Galileo had built a 20x telescope. This is when things got really interesting. He mapped stars in the night sky and tracked the movement of sunspots. He spotted the rings of Saturn, saw the craters of the Moon and discovered four moons orbiting Jupiter – Europa, Ganymede, Io and Callisto.

**Book good, book bad**
Galileo's observations proved that the Earth and other planets moved around the Sun. And that the Sun spun on its own axis – revolutionary! He wrote down what he learned in two books. The first, *The Starry Messenger*, was a bestseller. The second, *Dialogue*, got him into serious trouble.

Galileo's *Dialogue* book stayed on the Church's list of banned books for over 200 years.

RACE YOU TO THE BOTTOM!

**An arresting story**
Galileo was put on trial by the Church for his views on the universe in 1633. Found guilty, he was placed under house arrest for the rest of his life.

**A towering solution**
Galileo loved to prove the old ideas wrong. In his time, most scientists believed heavy objects fell faster than lighter ones. According to legend, Galileo proved otherwise by dropping one light and one much heavier cannonball from the top of the Leaning Tower of Pisa, Italy. Both reached the ground at the same time.

Galileo 1
Aristotle 0

**Galileo spacecraft**
Some 350 years after Galileo's death, the spacecraft named after him was launched by shuttle. The spacecraft entered Jupiter's atmosphere for a close-up look.

WANT MORE?

More on Galileo ✭ http://galileo.rice.edu/galileo.html

# STRANGE GAMES

The Olympic Games has two starting points, over 2600 years apart. In 776 BC, the ancient Greeks began holding a festival at Olympia every four years. The games lasted for about 1000 years until they were abolished by the Romans. In the 1880s, Frenchman Baron Pierre de Coubertin held the first modern Olympics in Athens. Seven out of the first eight Olympics were held in European cities, but the games are now a massive global event.

Baron Pierre de Coubertin

## ROPED IN

A popular event at early Olympics was the tug of war. In 1900, Edgar Aaybe, a journalist, was literally roped in when the Danish team found themselves a man short. The team won and Edgar became an unlikely gold medallist.

**Early errors**

Early Olympics would not have won gold for organisation. At the Paris 1900 games, Margaret Abbot won the women's golf competition but wasn't told. She lived the rest of her life not knowing she was an Olympic champ. At the 1920 games in Antwerp, Belgium, the cycle course ran across railway lines. Some cyclists had to stop at a level crossing for four minutes to let a train go past.

## EURO-LYMPICS: THEN AND NOW

**Greek games**
The ancient Greek Olympics started with just one sports event, a running race called a stade. Over time, events such as wrestling, javelin and long jump were added.

The reigning tug of war champs remain the City of London Police Force, winners in 1920. One of their team, Robert Spear, was banned for yanking the rope so hard that it pulled an opponent's arm out of its socket. Ouch!

**Odd events**
The Athens 1896 games featured rope climbing, one-handed weightlifting and a swimming race only for Greek sailors. The Paris 1900 games had hot-air ballooning, the horse long jump and the grisly sport of live pigeon shooting. The 1908 London games included the standing long jump (no run-up allowed) and motorboating.

Learn about the early games ☆ www.olympic.org/ancient-olympic-games

# BY THE POWER OF ODIN!

You're a humble peasant farmer in the 9th or 10th century, peacefully planting crops or tending your few chickens by the coast. Suddenly, something appears on the horizon... trouble with a capital 'V': it's a Viking raid! Before you know it, your village has been robbed, the church plundered and buildings burned down. Your best mates have been slaughtered or captured as slaves.

*Viking raiders on the rampage*

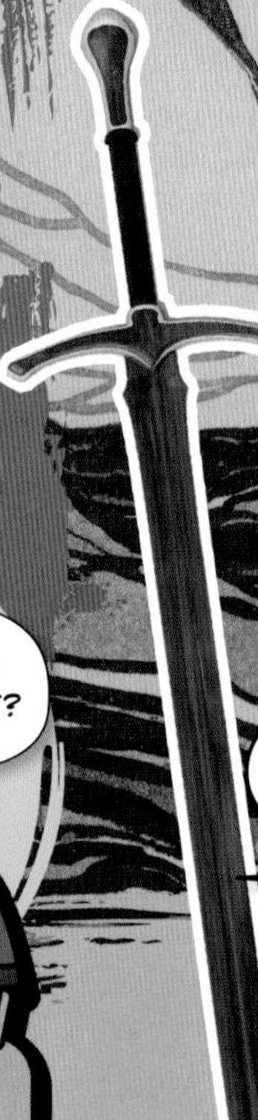

**Meet your enemy**

Vikings were warlike members of Norse peoples who lived in Scandinavia. For almost 300 years, they raided and invaded much of the coastline of northern Europe. They went into battle equipped with large swords or battleaxes, spears, shields and plenty of attitude.



**Lethal weapons**

Viking swords were 70–80cm (28–32in) long and double-edged. Owners often gave them names such as *Gramr* (Fierce) or *Fotbitr* (Leg-biter).

## BERSERKERS!

If you thought regular Viking warriors were bad enough, check out the Berserkers. These bear or wolfskin-clad nutters worked themselves up into a frenzy or ate drugged food before battle. Either way, they ran riot, oblivious to fear or pain. They truly believed they were invincible… and often were.

I SPY A NORSE BIT OF LAND AHEAD!

**Gods on their side**

The Vikings believed their Norse gods encouraged war. Thor, for example, was always on the warpath. His father, Odin, the main man, looked after Valhalla. This was the Vikings' heaven in the form of a giant feasting hall. Only Viking warriors who died gloriously in battle were allowed entry.

Odin on his eight-legged horse

## SURPRISE, SURPRISE

Viking raids were sudden and brutal. These Norse warriors were expert sailors and navigators. Their flat-bottomed longboats, propelled by sails and oars, could travel up rivers or shallow water at speed. Once onshore, Vikings attacked without delay, killing or stealing everything in their path.

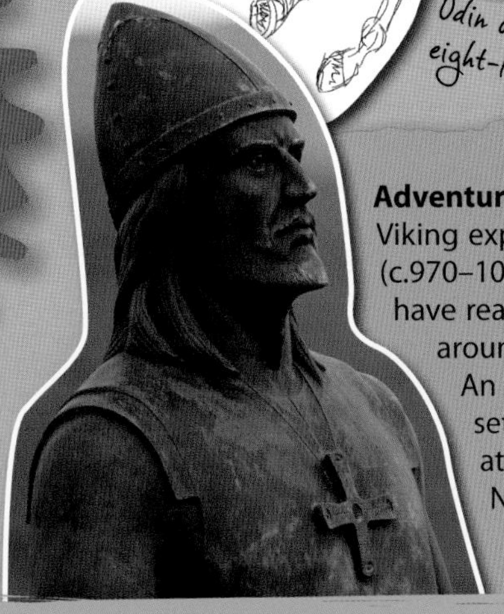

**Adventurous viking**

Viking explorer Leif Eriksson (c.970–1020) is believed to have reached North America around 1000 years ago. An 11th-century Viking settlement has been found at L'Anse aux Meadows in Newfoundland, Canada.

Statue of Leif Eriksson

WANT MORE?

Discover more about the Vikings ✯ www.jorvik-viking-centre.co.uk

# TOPPLED!

Between 1989 and 1991, Europe lost two countries (East Germany and the Soviet Union) and gained a whole lot more. The Soviet Union had been the world's largest superpower but in 1991, it dissolved into 15 different nations. Symbols of the Soviet Union, particularly its hammer and sickle flag, and many statues of Soviet leaders, were toppled or destroyed.

**Tear down the wall**
As the Soviet Union eased its grip on eastern Europe, East Germany and West Germany were reunited as one country. The Berlin Wall, which had split the city in two for almost 30 years, was torn down with relish by Germans.

Germans old and young became Mauerspechte - wall woodpeckers. They chiselled out chunks of the Berlin Wall as souvenirs.

**Gor blimey**
Mikhail Gorbachev was born in 1931. He became Soviet President in 1985. Gorbachev introduced reforms including glasnost which saw more freedoms for people. He removed Soviet troops from eastern European countries such as Hungary and East Germany.

## WE'RE FREE!

In September 1991, the three Baltic states of Latvia, Estonia and Lithuania broke away from the Soviet Union. They became independent again after being swallowed up by the Soviets in 1944. Statues of former Soviet leaders such as Josef Stalin and Vladimir Lenin were toppled.

A map of eastern Europe after the Soviet Union broke up in 1991.

Toppled statue of Vladimir Lenin in Vilnius, Lithuania.

**Statue park**
More than 20 years on, a theme park in Lithuania has turned back time. It features over 80 rescued statues of Soviet leaders along with actors playing roles of communist party workers and Soviet guards. Sounds grim, but over 200,000 visit each year!

Stalin lying in Vilnius, Lithuania.

WANT MORE?

**Mikhail Gorbachev won the Nobel Peace Prize in 1990.**

# THE PRANCING HORSE

Europe is the home of many legendary sports cars from Lamborghini in Italy to Porsche in Germany. Few are more famous than Ferrari. The super-sleek vehicles, mostly in racing red, were the brainchild of a speed freak called Enzo Ferrari (1898–1988). He began his adult life as a blacksmith in the Italian Army during World War I.

Enzo Ferrari in his eight-cylinder Alfa Romeo, 1924.

**Childhood dreams**

Enzo Ferrari was ten when he saw his first motor race and decided that a life of speed was for him. He nearly didn't make it, though. In 1916, he almost died of flu. Then, in 1919, while driving to his first race Enzo's car got stuck in a blizzard, and he was chased by a pack of wolves. Luckily, he scared them off with shots from a revolver he kept under his carseat.

## BADGE OF HONOUR

In 1923, Enzo won a race at Ravenna in Italy. It was watched by the mother of Count Francesco Baracca, a World War I fighter pilot. She asked Enzo to use the symbol painted on her son's plane for good luck. Today, all Ferraris come with the famous black prancing horse on a yellow background. Yellow is the colour of Ferrari's home city of Modena.

**Racing and riding**
To begin with, Ferrari's race teams drove Alfa Romeos. But Enzo began to make his own sports cars after World War II. Ferrari also ran his own Formula One team which has since won over 200 races and 31 world championships.

In 2012, 964 Ferrari cars, the most ever in one place, roared around the Silverstone race circuit in the UK.

## GTO TO GO

One of the most exclusive Ferraris of all was the Ferrari 250 GTO. Only 39 of these were made between 1962 and 1964. In 2012, two of these rare vehicles were sold, one for £20.2 million (US$31.2 million) and another for £2 million more.

SOLD £20.2 million

In 1985, a sales brochure for a Ferrari 250 GTO car sold for £1070 (US$1627).

# THE EMPEROR OF ELBA

Napoleon Bonaparte (1769–1821) was a mighty general and Emperor of France. He was the most feared man in Europe until, in April 1814, he was forced to sign away his power. The Treaty of Fontainebleau saw him exiled to Elba, a small island in the Mediterranean Sea. France appointed a new ruler, King Louis XVIII, and Europe moved on. Napoleon, nicknamed Boney by British troops, appeared to be yesterday's man… but was he?

WE'LL FOLLOW. BONEY'S BACK!

Napoleon's first wife was called Rose but he didn't like the name, so called her Josephine instead.

**Exiled in Elba**

Napoleon tried to improve life on Elba. He surveyed the land, ordered hospitals to be built and drilled his tiny army of several hundred loyal soldiers who accompanied him from France. His mother and sister joined him in exile but his wife, Marie Louise, refused. What a spoilsport!

**Escape from Elba**

About 300 days after he arrived, Napoleon gave Elba the elbow. There were spies on the island and ships from other countries keeping watch around the coast. But Napoleon and a handful of his loyal guards managed to escape by grabbing a ship and sailing to the French coast.

**March to power**

Napoleon marched towards Paris, his tiny force swelling into a large army. Many Frenchmen remained big fans. French soldiers were sent to capture him at Grenoble, but instead joined forces with him. As he arrived in Paris, in March 1815, King Louis XVIII fled to Belgium. Boney was back!

## WATERLOO

Napoleon again threatened to conquer Europe but his opponents joined forces. British and Prussian armies defeated him at the Battle of Waterloo, in June 1815. It was game over for Boney! He was exiled again, but given no power. This time, he was sent to the isolated island of St Helena, in the middle of the Atlantic Ocean, for the rest of his life.

St Helena is 1900km (1180mi) west of Angola.

Over a third of Napoleon's 72,000 troops at Waterloo were killed or wounded.

**Pain in the behind**

By the time of Waterloo, Napoleon suffered terribly from painful haemorrhoids. These made it uncomfortable for him to sit on a horse.

WANT MORE?

Find out more ✫ www.ngv.vic.gov.au/napoleon/facts-and-figures/did-you-know

# CURIOUS CUSTOMS

Which country smashes crockery to see in the New Year?* Where would you find an ornamental green pickle placed last on a Christmas tree?* And what part of a bridegroom's clothing is cut to pieces during many Italian weddings?* All these and many, many more strange customs and traditions occur in different countries throughout Europe.

Cacti stand guard outside a Greek home.

Evil eye

**Good and bad luck**

The Irish Celts considered a four-leafed clover a lucky charm. Greeks place cacti near the front door to ward off bad things. For 3000 years in Turkey, evil eye glass beads have decorated anything that may cause envy in others, from a new dress to a car. The aim is to ward off evil spirits.

**A smashing time**

In Germany, the night before a couple marry, friends turn up with plates, cups and other goods. They smash the items to bring good luck to the marriage. This is called *Polterabend*. The couple are left to clean up the mess!

WHAT THE DEVIL'S THE CORRECT TIME?

## CLOCK WISE

Most churches in Malta have two clocks but set to different times. It's not a time zone thing. One clock tells the wrong time to confuse the devil, should he turn up.

***Answers:** 1. Denmark 2. Germany 3. The bridegroom's tie.

**Bad Santa**

In Austria, Slovenia and other parts of central Europe, Krampus is Santa's far-from-friendly alter ego. People go out wearing devil-like masks. They snarl and rattle chains to frighten children who have misbehaved before Christmas.

**Pooping log!**

This is the name given to a Catalan custom in Spain. From 8 December, a hollowed-out log is 'fed' with sweets, fruits and nuts. It's then beaten with sticks on Christmas Eve or Day, so that the log poops out the treasures inside.

**Spider inside**

In the Ukraine, finding a spider's web on Christmas morning is said to bring good luck. So Ukrainians decorate their Christmas trees with fake webs and spiders.

More customs ✯ www.traditionscustoms.com/christmas-traditions/christmas-europe

# PLAGUE!

The Black Death was the deadliest wave of disease to strike medieval Europe. It was a massive epidemic of the plague virus caused by bacteria carried by fleas that lived on rats. The outbreak is thought to have begun in Asia and been carried by traders to the Mediterranean. It reached Sicily in 1347 and, for six years, swept through Europe with devastating effects.

In London, England, it's still illegal for someone with the plague to take a taxi ride without telling the driver!

**Way to go**

Not everyone who caught the plague died, but those who did suffered horribly. Terrible fevers and pains in the back and limbs were often accompanied by large swellings all over their body. Dark purple or black blotches appeared on the skin from bleeding inside the body. Many victims seemed to go mad or coughed up blood before dying.

**GROSS!**

Cities such as Paris, Hamburg and Florence lost over half of their people to the Black Death.

**Dim doctors**
The disease and how it spread was not understood at all. In France, the Parisian Medical Faculty told people not to wash for fear that water would weaken their hearts! In reality, the filthy conditions found in many medieval towns helped the Black Death spread like wildfire.

outhern Russia
45

From Asia

2000 AD

**Doctor death**
Plague doctors tried to treat the sick. Some doctors wore heavy coats smeared in wax or raw sheep or beef fat. Their masks with long beaks were stuffed with straw, herbs and scented flowers to ward off the stench of death.

BLACK DEATH TOLL: at least **30** million

IT WASN'T ME.

OR ME . . .

GULP!

DOG 1355614

CAT 8167102

RAT 3690231

**Dirty dogs**
Dogs and cats were killed as many people thought they were spreading the disease. But this just removed many of the animals that would have preyed on the disease-spreading rats.

WANT MORE?

**Some docs put live chickens on Black Death swellings to cure them – it didn't work!**

# ERUPTING EUROPE

It's AD 79. The 20,000 or so residents of the bustling Roman town of Pompeii (near Naples) were going about their business when disaster struck. Mount Vesuvius – a nearby volcano – began erupting. When Vesuvius blew, it blew big, spewing out over 1.3 million tonnes (1.4 million tons) of molten rock and ash every second for six of the most violent hours on Earth.

BAD BOY STROMBOLI

Archaeologists found the entire ancient Roman town of Pompeii perfectly preserved under the hardened ash layer.

Excavation of Pompeii

## FROZEN IN STONE

Pompeii and the neighbouring town of Herculaneum were bombarded by the eruption. The towns were left covered in a layer of ash up to 25m (82ft) deep. Pompeii wasn't rediscovered for another 1700 years, when it became an archaeological marvel.

Pompeii with Mount Vesuvius in the background.

Stromboli fires jets and fountains of red-hot molten rock from its lava-filled central crater. It's been doing this almost continuously for 2000 years.

**Home of Vulcan**
Vesuvius, along with Etna and Stromboli, are Italy's three bad boys. They're all volcanoes that have erupted in the last century. Mount Etna is where the ancient Greeks believed their god of fire, Vulcan, lived. That's where we get the word volcano from.

**Lava land**
Apart from Italy, Europe's other volcanic hotspot is Iceland, home to 31 active volcanoes. In 2010, Eyjafjallajökull erupted big time, sending over 300 million tonnes (305 million tons) of ash 9km (5.5mi) up into the atmosphere. The ash could clog up jet engines, so over 100,000 flights had to be cancelled.

TURN BACK!

9km (5.5miles)

300 million tonnes

Plaster casts were taken of some of Pompeii's victims.

Two of Pompeii's fallen figures

**In a steam**
It may be chilly outside, but bathers in Iceland's Blue Lagoon are toasty warm. This giant pool, not far from the capital, Reykjavik, is filled with piping-hot water heated by volcanic activity deep underground.

ANYONE SEEN MY SOAP?

Blue Lagoon, Iceland

WANT MORE?

**Today, over 2.5 million people visit Pompeii and all its exhibits each year.**

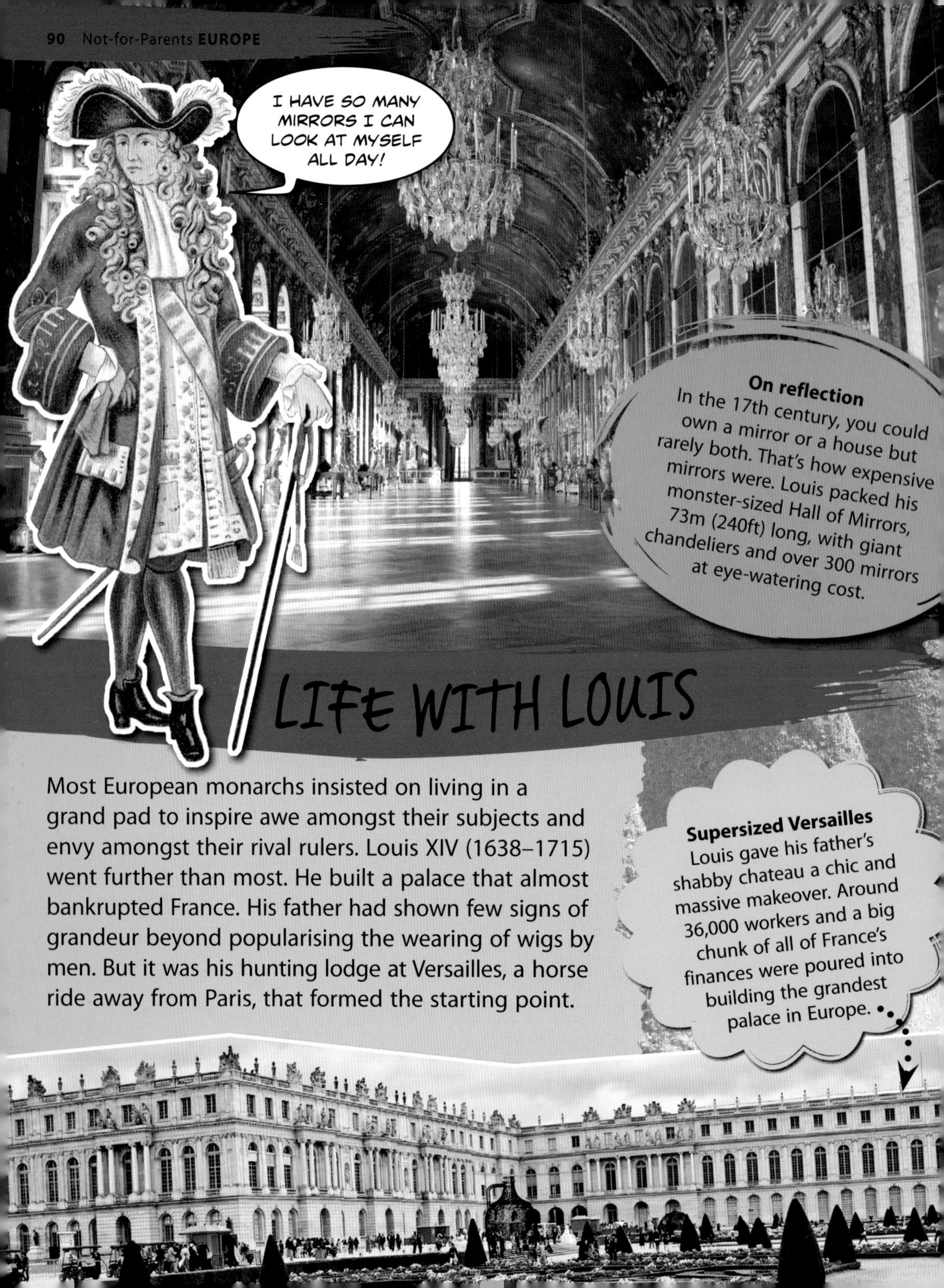


**On reflection**
In the 17th century, you could own a mirror or a house but rarely both. That's how expensive mirrors were. Louis packed his monster-sized Hall of Mirrors, 73m (240ft) long, with giant chandeliers and over 300 mirrors at eye-watering cost.

# LIFE WITH LOUIS

Most European monarchs insisted on living in a grand pad to inspire awe amongst their subjects and envy amongst their rival rulers. Louis XIV (1638–1715) went further than most. He built a palace that almost bankrupted France. His father had shown few signs of grandeur beyond popularising the wearing of wigs by men. But it was his hunting lodge at Versailles, a horse ride away from Paris, that formed the starting point.

**Supersized Versailles**
Louis gave his father's shabby chateau a chic and massive makeover. Around 36,000 workers and a big chunk of all of France's finances were poured into building the grandest palace in Europe.

## GRAND GROUNDS

The gardens of Versailles are four times the size of Monaco. They contain 200,000 trees, 400 sculptures, a full-sized canal and vast fountains supplied by 35km (22mi) of water pipes.

**x 200,000**

**x 400**

**35km (22mi) pipes**

About 210,000 flowers and plants are planted in Versailles' gardens every year.

**All about him**
Louis adopted the Sun as his symbol, seen here on a fence at Versailles. He was known as the Sun King because it was said all of France revolved around him. Now that is self-centred!

### PALACE TOP TRUMPS

| | |
|---|---|
| ROOMS: | 700 |
| STAIRCASES: | 67 |
| FIREPLACES: | 1200 |
| WINDOWS: | 2000 |
| STABLES: | For over 10,000 horses |
| COST: | Off the scale! |

**Causing a stink**
For all his finery and etiquette, Louis stank. It's believed he only had three baths in his whole 76-year lifetime!

WANT MORE?

**A fifth of the government's income went on running Versailles during Louis XIV's reign.**

# NO BUSINESS LIKE SNOW BUSINESS

Snow falls heavily in many parts of Europe so it's no surprise that people have always found ways to get around. Ancient skis dating back more than 5000 years have been found in Norway, Russia and Sweden. Skiing or skating for fun or sport is a more recent invention, as are some of these more peculiar winter pastimes.

**Ski flying**

Norwegian teenager Olaf Rye made the first-known ski jump in 1809. He covered a distance of 9.5m (31ft). Today's ski jumpers travel ten times that distance from giant ramps.

Ski flying takes ski jumping to extremes. In Norway, in 2011, Johan Remen Evensen completed a whopping world record jump of 246.5m (809ft) – that's two and a half soccer pitches long!

Slovenia's Robert Kranjec has made 140 jumps each over 200m (656ft). That's serious ski flying!

## SAIL AWAY

The Netherlands, Poland, Czech Republic and many other parts of Europe have lots of lakes that freeze over in winter. These provide the perfect spot for ice yachts. These special yachts use skates or ski-like runners to skim across the ice, whipped along by the winter winds.

Ice yachts can top speeds of 100km/h (62mph).

Ice sailors wear life jackets... just in case they travel over thin ice and end up in water.

## FLYING PAN

Wok racing? Yes, that's right. Kitchen woks with a reinforced bottom are sent hurtling down super-fast, ice-covered bobsled runs. Not on their own of course – that would be madness. Instead they carry a wok racer – a brave soul dressed in ice-hockey gear for protection.

In 2009 at the 1300m (4265ft) long Winterberg bobsled track, George Hackl hit 105.4km/h (65.6mph) - in a wok!

Check out those cooking ladles on his feet - they act as mini woks!

WANT MORE?

See more ✯ www.mnn.com/health/fitness-well-being/photos/12-wacky-winter-sports

# INDEX

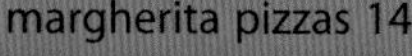
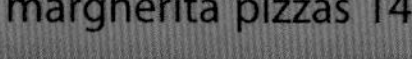
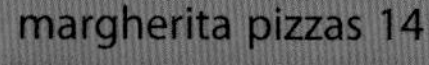

NOT-FOR-PARENTS
# EUROPE
## EVERYTHING YOU EVER WANTED TO KNOW

**1st Edition**
**Published September 2013**

WELDONOWEN

Conceived by Weldon Owen in partnership with Lonely Planet
Produced by Weldon Owen Limited
An imprint of Red Lemon Press Limited
Northburgh House,
10 Northburgh Street
London, EC1V 0AT, UK


Project managed and commissioned by Dynamo Ltd
**Project manager** Alison Gadsby
**Project editor** Melanie Hibbert
**Designer** Clair Lansley
**Picture researcher** Sarah Ross
**Indexer** Marie Lorimer

**Published by**
Lonely Planet Publications Pty Ltd ABN 36 005 607 983
90 Maribyrnong St, Footscray, Victoria 3011, Australia

ISBN 978-1-74321-913-3

Printed and bound in China by 1010 Printing Int Ltd
9 8 7 6 5 4 3 2 1



**www.redlemonpress.com**

Red Lemon Press Limited is part of the Bonnier Publishing Group
**www.bonnierpublishing.com**

**Credits and acknowledgments**

KEY – tl top left, tc top centre, tr top right, cl centre left, c centre, cr centre right, bl bottom left, bc bottom centre, br bottom right.

All images © Shutterstock except:
8br, 16tr, 28tr, 51cl, 55cr, 57br, 68bl **Alamy**; 12bc, 14tr, 16cl, 22tr, 30tr, 30bl, 31tr, 32tr, 33tr, 33cr, 33bl, 41br, 42t, 49tr, 53cl, 53cr, 61bl, 64tr, 65tc, 66bc, 67bl, 75br, 76tr, 76cl, 80bl, 82tr, 82br, 83br, 85tr, 92tl Corbis; 12tr, 12cl, 12br, 13tr **courtesy of The Ice Bar**; 44cl **courtesy of Legoland**; 8tr, 8cl, 9br, 10tr, 10cl, 11c, 13cl, 15tl, 17cl, 17br, 19cl, 22br, 24br, 26cr, 27br, 36tr, 37tr, 39bl, 44tr, 46tr, 46br, 47tr, 48c, 50tr, 50bl, 52bc, 55tr, 56cl, 58tr, 58c, 58br, 59br, 62cl, 64bl, 65bl, 70tr, 70cr, 71bl, 72t, 72bc, 74tr, 75bl, 78cr, 79bl, 79br, 81br, 93br **Getty Images**; 15bl, 69tr,15tr **Rex Features.**

Cover illustrations by **Chris Corr**

**LONELY PLANET OFFICES**

**Australia Head Office**
Locked Bag 1, Footscray, Victoria 3011
Phone 03 8379 8000 Fax 03 8379 8111

**USA**
150 Linden St, Oakland, CA 94607
Phone 510 250 6400 Toll free 800 275 8555 Fax 510 893 8572

**UK**
Media Centre, 201 Wood Lane, London W12 7TQ
Phone 020 8433 1333 Fax 020 8702 0112

**lonelyplanet.com/contact**

Paper in this book is certified against the Forest Stewardship Council™ standards. FSC™ promotes environmentally responsible, socially beneficial and economically viable management of the world's forests.